Spelling Rules!

Janelle Ho and
Helen Pearson

STUDENT BOOK K

NSW Edition

Name: ______________________________

Class: ______________________________

Spelling Rules! Student Book K
NSW Edition
ISBN: 978 0 6550 9257 5

Publisher: Catherine Charles-Brown
Designer and typesetter: Trish Hayes
Illustrator: Stephen Michael King
Series editor: Marie James
Indigenous consultant: Al Fricker

This edition published in 2023 by Matilda Education Australia, an imprint of Meanwhile Education Pty Ltd Melbourne, Australia
T: 1300 277 235
E: customersupport@matildaed.com.au
www.matildaeducation.com.au

First edition published in 2006 by Macmillan Science and Education Australia Pty Ltd

Printed in China by Central
Sep-2022

NOTE TO TEACHERS AND PARENTS

Spelling Rules!

Some students are natural spellers. But the vast majority of students need formal, systematic and sequential instruction about the way spelling works and the strategies they can use to become independent, confident spellers and spelling risk-takers.

The *Spelling Rules!* program is based on sound linguistic and pedagogical theory. It is informed by research into how students of different ages acquire and apply spelling skills, and how those skills move from the working to the long-term memory. The program closely follows the NSW English Curriculum. NSW Curriculum references are provided in the Teacher Resource Books. The program consists of seven Student Books, fully supported by two Teacher Resource Books.

Each student book contains units of work, with each unit designed to be used over the course of a week. The content of each unit follows the suggested instructional sequence in the NSW English syllabus. Each unit simultaneously develops new skills and reinforces skills from previous units. Where appropriate, topic words from other curriculum areas such as mathematics, science and social sciences are included. When spelling rules and tips are introduced, only known sounds and letter patterns are used so that students focus on one skill at a time. Regular revision units enable teachers to assess student progress and reinforce key rules and patterns from previous units.

Spelling knowledge

Learning to spell involves developing different kinds of spelling knowledge:

- **Kinaesthetic knowledge** – the physical feeling when saying different sounds and words, and when writing the shapes of letters and words
- **Phonological knowledge** – how a word sounds and the patterns of sounds in words
- **Visual knowledge** – how letters and words look and the visual patterns in words
- **Morphemic knowledge** – the meaning or function of words or parts of words
- **Etymological knowledge** – the origins and history of words and the effect this has on spelling patterns.

Icons used in Student Book K

The following icons identify the main spelling strategy that students will use to complete an activity.

Say the word. (Kinaesthetic knowledge) These activities ask students to experience how sounds feel in the mouth and jaw. Changing the positions of the jaw, lips, and tongue changes the sounds we make. Encourage students to pronounce the sounds and words accurately. If they mispronounce a sound or word, they may misrepresent it in writing.

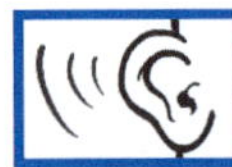

Listen to the word. (Phonological knowledge) These activities focus on discriminating between different sounds and breaking up words into syllables or individual sound segments (phonemes).

Look at the word. (Visual knowledge) These activities help students to see how the sound is represented using combinations of letters, and to associate this visual pattern with what they are hearing. Students will develop the ability to know when a word does or does not 'look right'.

Understand the word. (Morphemic and etymological knowledge) These activities focus on word meanings, word families, prefixes and suffixes, spelling rules, word origins and so on – all of which help embed spelling in the long-term memory.

Practise writing the word. (Kinaesthetic knowledge) These activities develop students' awareness of the physical movement involved in writing the word. By practising writing the word a number of times and in different contexts, the spelling becomes embedded in the long-term memory.

This icon highlights useful spelling rules.

This icon tells students that a special clue or hint is provided for an activity. It may be a spelling, grammar or punctuation convention, or a definition of a useful term.

Spelling Rules! Student Book K (ISBN 9780655092575) © Janelle Ho, Helen Pearson/Matilda Education Australia

Student Book K

Units of work

The NSW edition of *Student Book K* contains 38 weekly units of work. You would probably start using the workbook around week 3 of the first year at school, once other routines are settled. Each unit focuses on one or more consonants or vowels. In this revised edition, students start to combine sounds from Unit 2 with high-frequency sight words introduced from Unit 2 onwards. In addition to common digraphs and split digraphs, the plural (s) and tense-marking (*ed, ing*) suffixes for simple regular words are taught. Common homophones are also introduced. See the **Scope and Sequence** chart on the inside front cover for more information.

Word lists

From Unit 2 onwards, every unit includes a short word list. The words enable students to focus on the letter pattern, sound pattern, or etymological or morphological element being taught in the unit. They are selected to support the learning focus and spelling strategies.

Some words are provided with traceable letters. These words allow students to begin practising high-frequency sight words. By the end of Book K, students will have been introduced to almost all the high-frequency sight words they need for reading and writing.

Unit at a glance

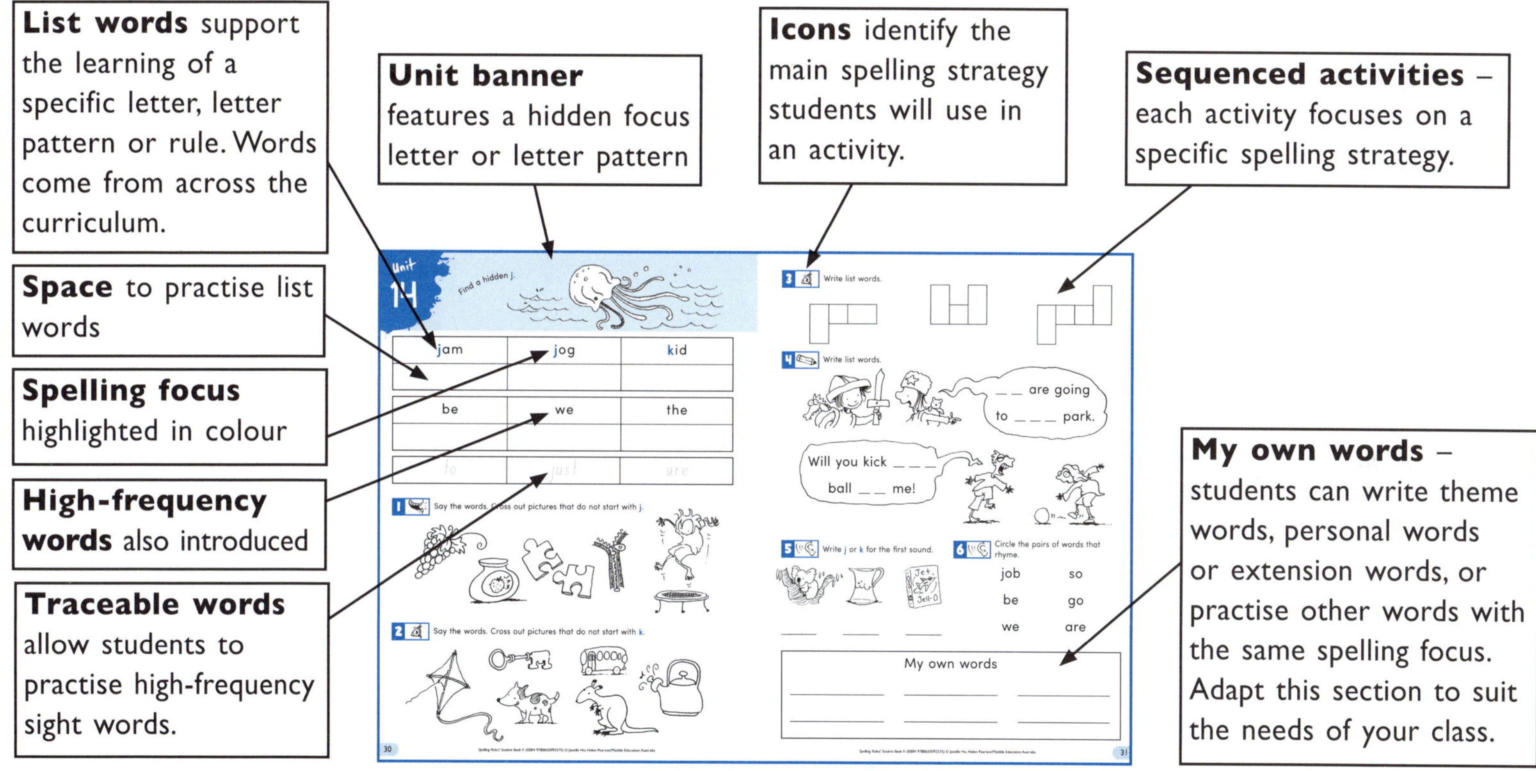

Spelling Rules! Teacher Resource Book K–2

Full teacher support for *Student Book K* is provided by *Spelling Rules! Teacher Resource Book K–2*. Here you will find valuable background information about spelling development and spelling knowledge, along with practical resources, such as:

- teaching tips for every unit in *Student Book K*
- extra word lists
- strategies for teaching spelling
- guidelines for assessing spelling and diagnosing spelling errors
- activities to support struggling spellers
- worthwhile extension for more able spellers.

Unit 1

1 What letter can you see in the pictures? Write the letter.

 ____________

 ____________

2 Circle the letter that makes the first sound.

a

p

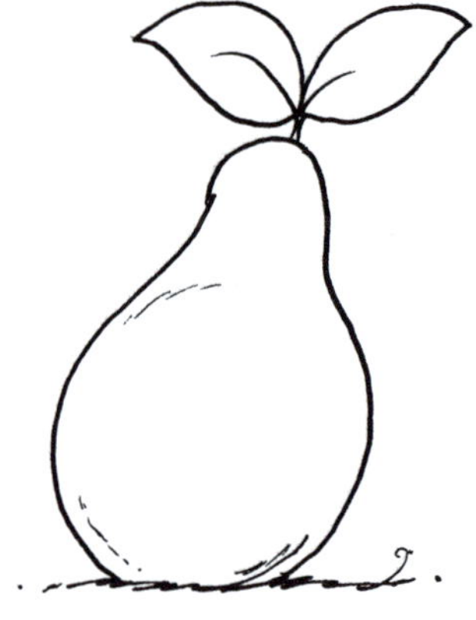

p

t

a

t

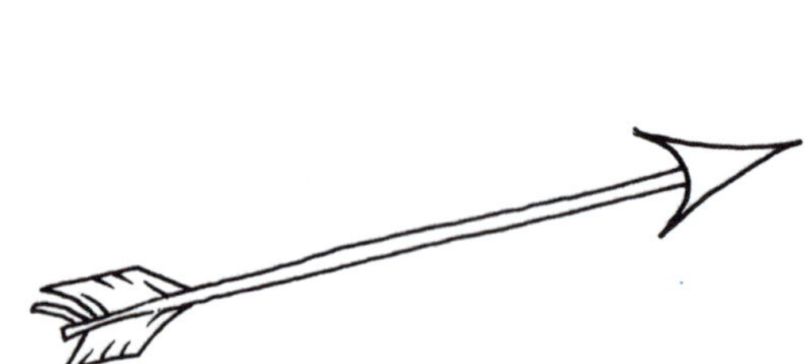

a

p

s

p

a

t

Colour the shapes with **p**.
What do you see? ________

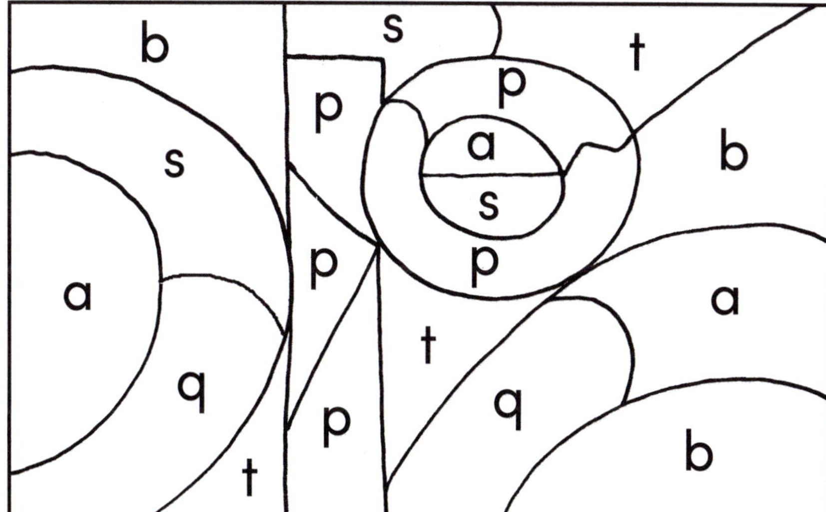

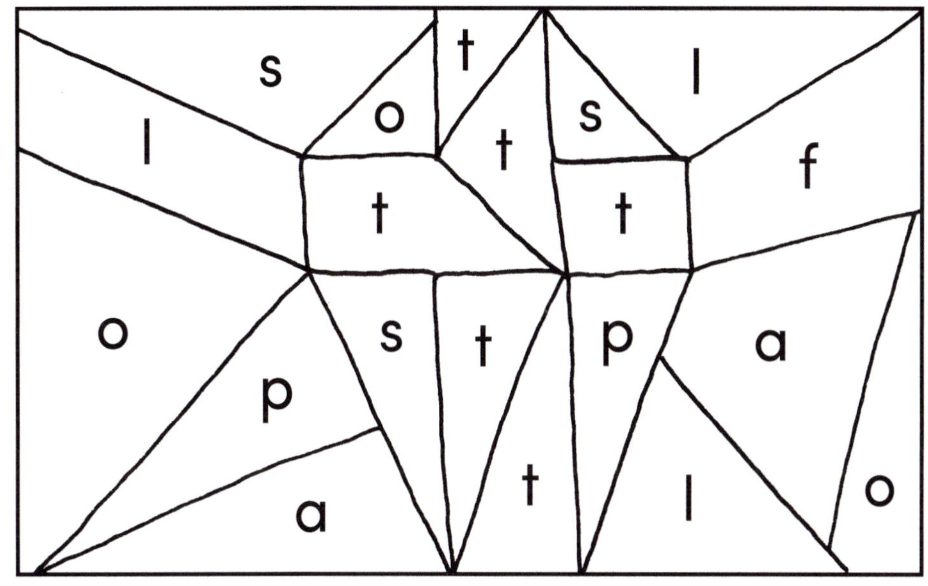

Colour the shapes with **t**.
What do you see? ________

Write the letter that makes the first sound.

________	________
________	________
________	________

Unit 2

Find a hidden t.

pat	sat	tap
a	at	as

1 Say each word. Write the last sound you hear.

s  ____  ____  ____

t  ____  ____  ____

p  ____  ____ 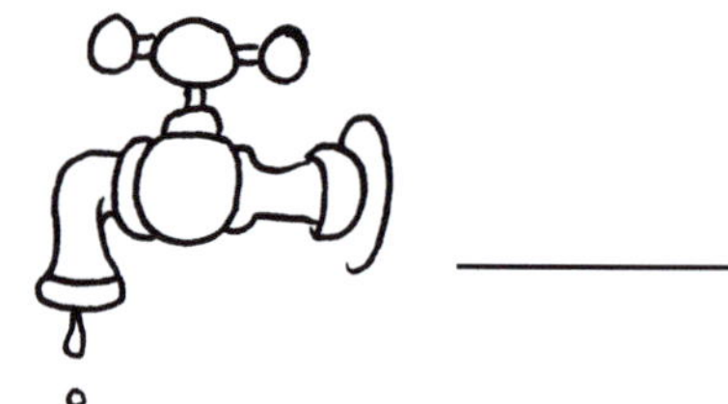 ____

2 Write the missing letter.

 r _ t

 h _ t

 c _ t

m _ t

Spelling Rules! Student Book K (ISBN 9780655092575) © Janelle Ho, Helen Pearson/Matilda Education Australia

Colour the picture if you hear **a** in the middle.

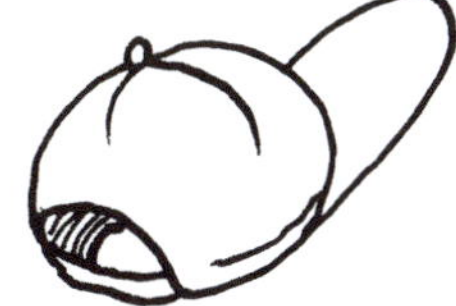

Circle **a**, **at** and **as**.

There is a man at the door.

That rat is as fat as a cat.

I like to tap as I count.

5 Colour **p** in blue. Colour **t** in red. Colour **a** in yellow. Colour **s** in green.

My own words

______________	______________	______________
______________	______________	______________

Unit 3

Find a hidden c.

cat	cap	gap
sag	gag	gas

1 What letter can you see in the picture? Write the letter.

___

___

2 Say each word. Write the letter that makes the first sound.

c

g

___  ___ 

___  ___ 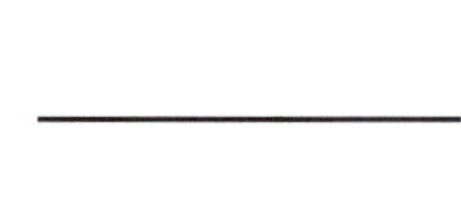

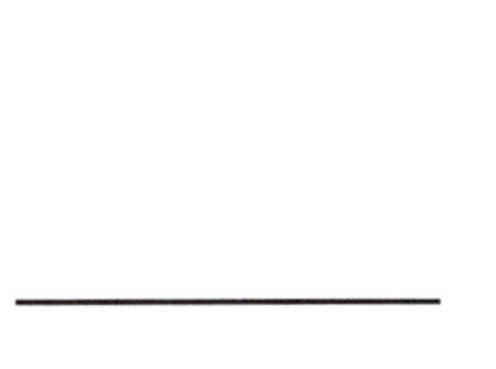

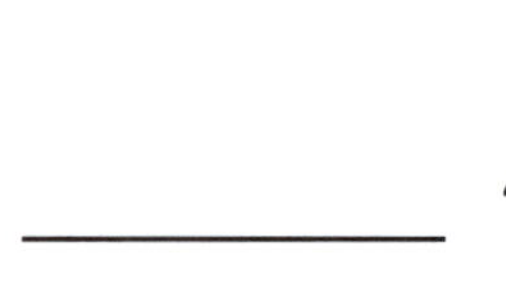

___ 

___  ___ 

Say each word. Write the letter that makes the last sound.

 ______

 ______

 ______

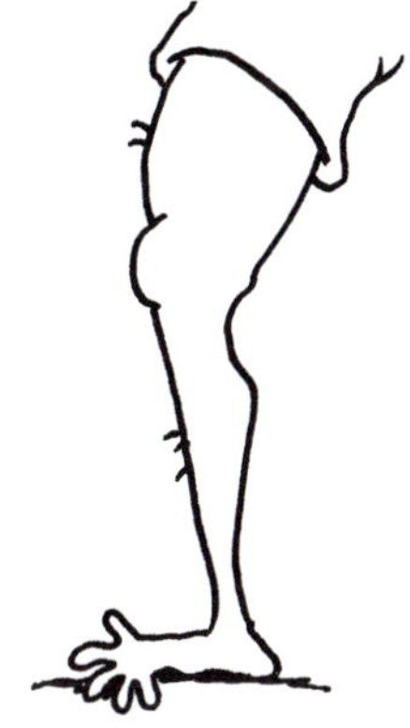 ______

Write list words.

I see a  in a 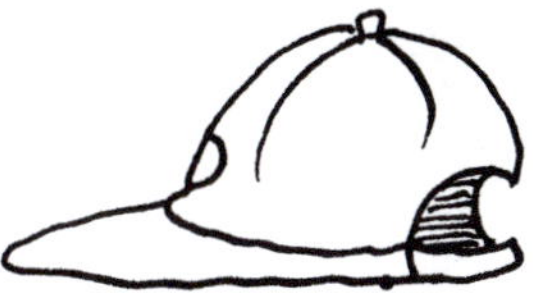

_ _ _   _ _ _

Sam's smile has a .

_ _ _

My own words

______ ______ ______

______ ______ ______

Unit 4

Find a hidden **m**.

mat	**m**ap	**i**t	**i**s

am	sip	in	I

1 Say the words. Write **i** or **m** for the first sound.

2 Colour the shapes with **i**.

What do you see?

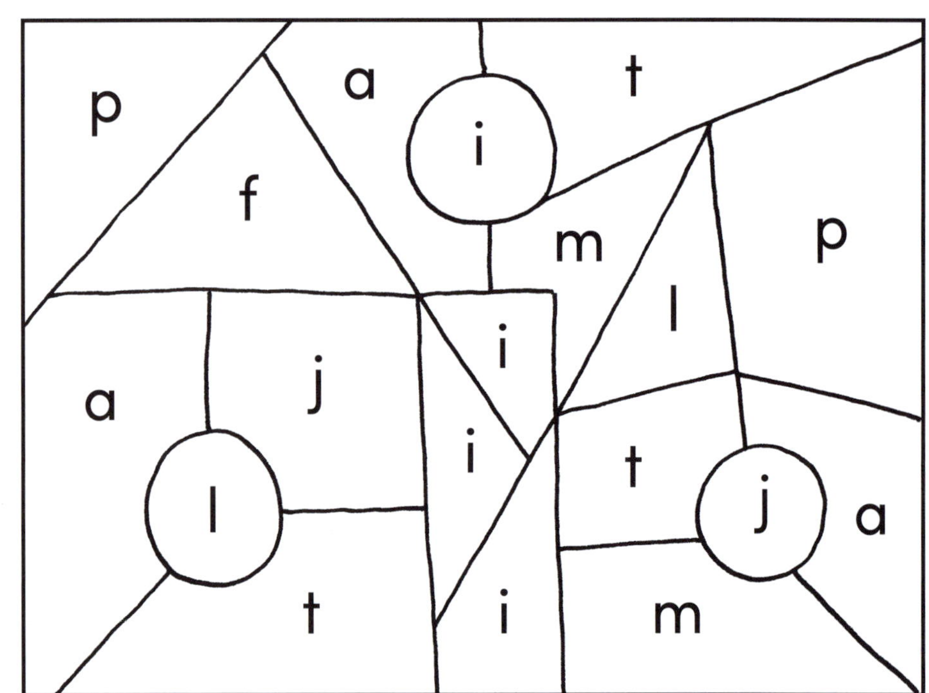

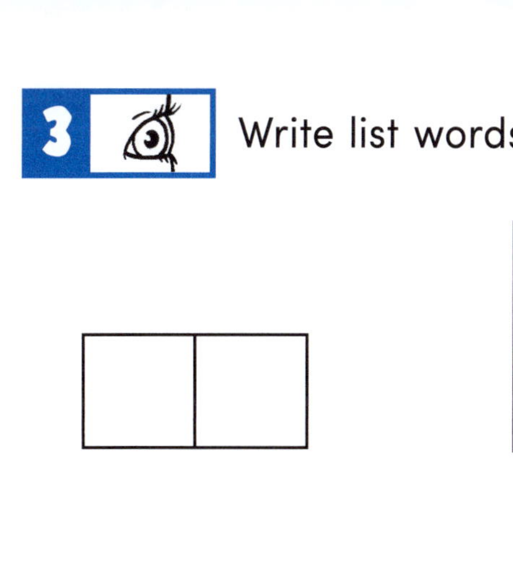

Write list words.

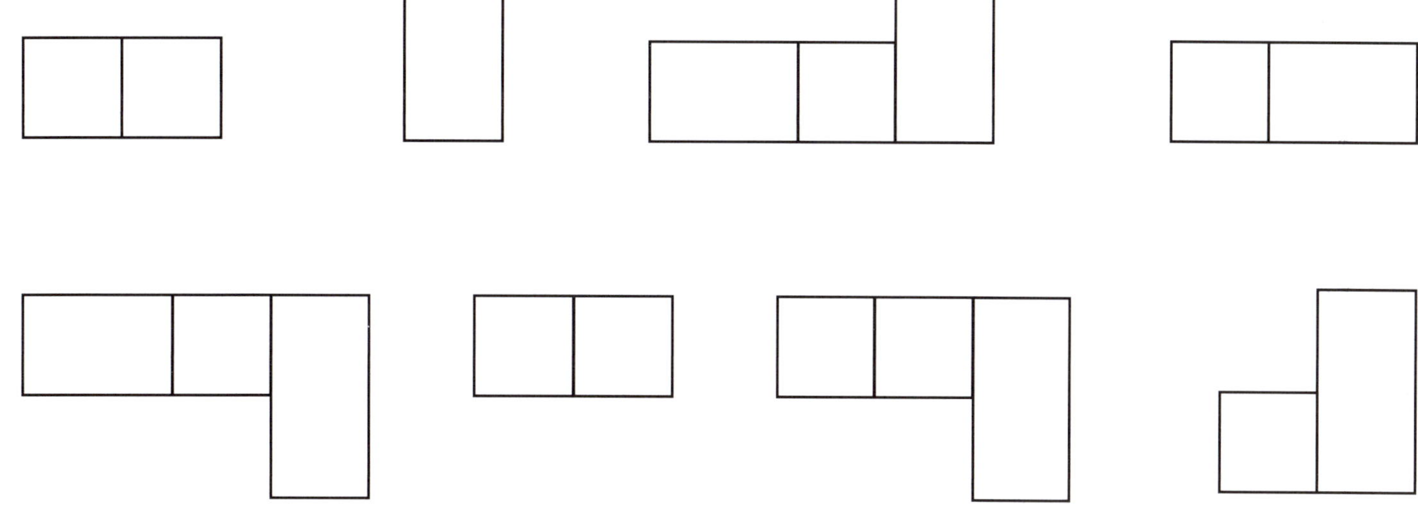

Write list words.

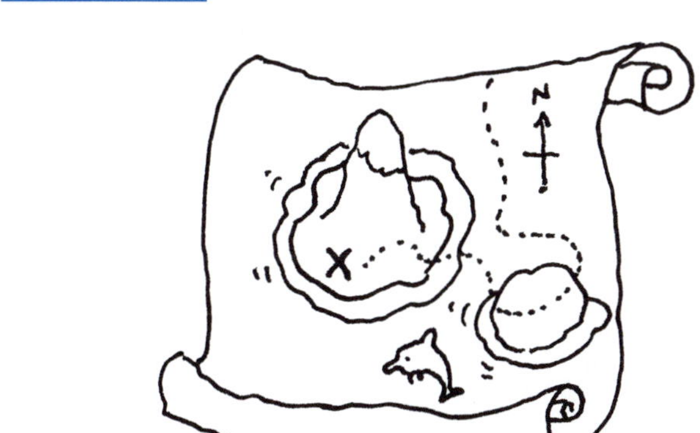

What is it?

It is a ___ ___ ___.

What is it?

It ___ ___ a ___ ___ ___.

My own words

______________ ______________ ______________

______________ ______________ ______________

Unit 5

Find a hidden **n**.

no	**n**ap	**n**ip	ti**n**

on	man	cats	pins

1 Write different list words.

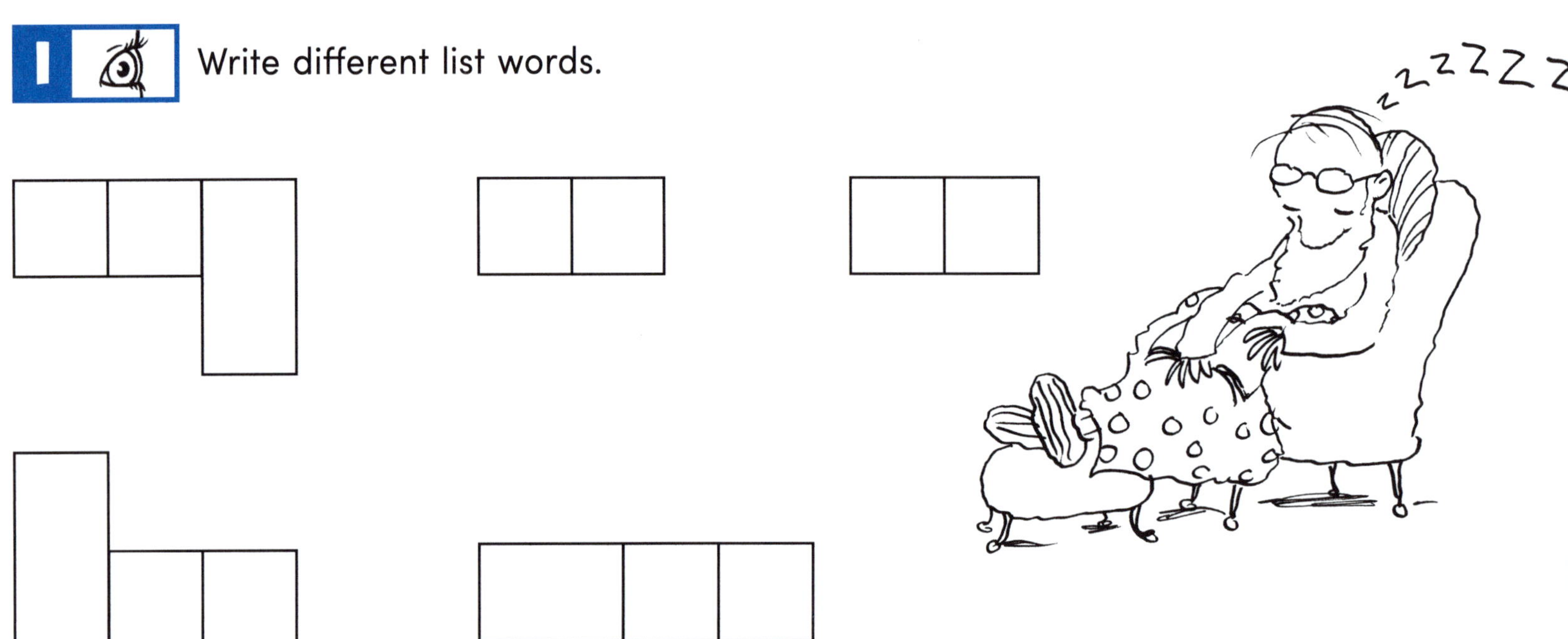

2 Write the letter that makes the first sound.

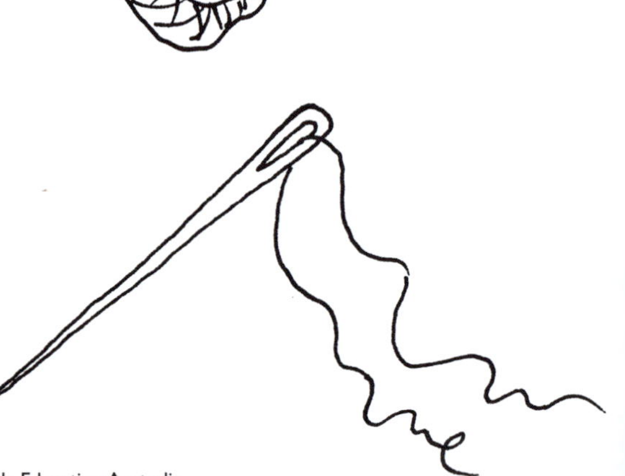

Spelling Rules! Student Book K (ISBN 9780655092575) © Janelle Ho, Helen Pearson/Matilda Education Australia

 Make words with the same first sound.

a < n ____________
a < m ____________

n < ip ____________
n < ap ____________

Most words add **s** to show there is more than one.

cat → cats *pin → pins*

 Write the list words backwards to make a new word.

nap ____________ nip ____________

on ____________ tin ____________

 Add **s** to show more than one.

2 mat __

3 friend __

4 cup __

5 rat __

My own words

____________ ____________ ____________

____________ ____________ ____________

Unit 6

Find a hidden l.

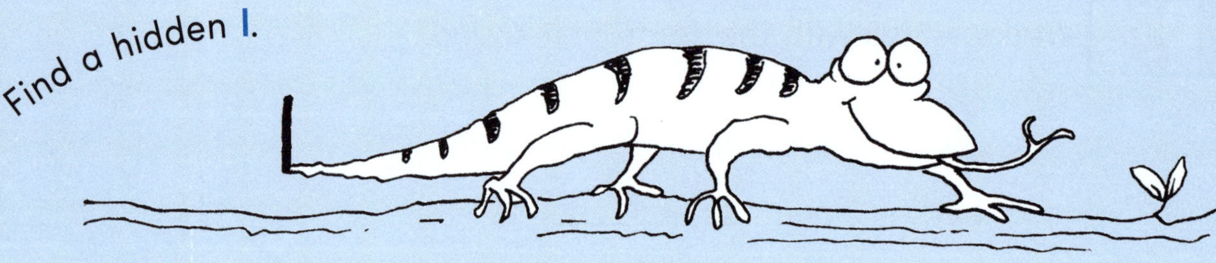

dig	lip	lap	pal

dip	dad	do	did

1 Colour the pictures starting with **d** red. Colour the pictures starting with **l** blue.

2 Draw lines to join the rhyming words.

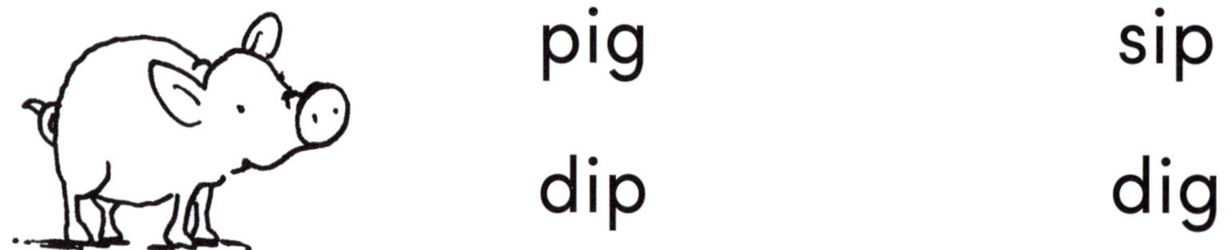

pig sip

dip dig

3 Make words with different last sounds.

di < p ________ / g ________

si < t ________ / p ________

Spelling Rules! Student Book K (ISBN 9780655092575) © Janelle Ho, Helen Pearson/Matilda Education Australia

4 Change one letter to make a new word.

lⓐp	______	sⓘt	______
tⓐp	______	pⓘt	______
ⓐt	______	dⓘd	______

5 Write the missing letters.

D__ __ you
d__ your
spelling?

I d__ __,
D__ __.

My own words

______ ______ ______

______ ______ ______

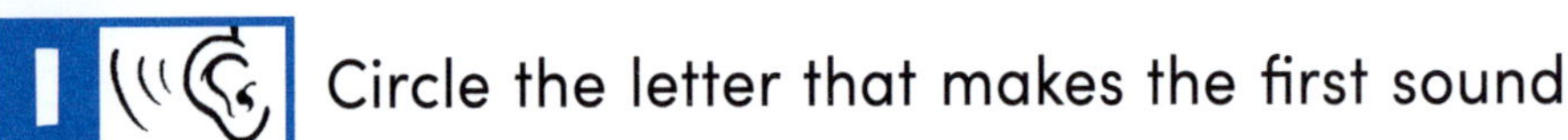

1 Circle the letter that makes the first sound.

d t

d g

m n

p d

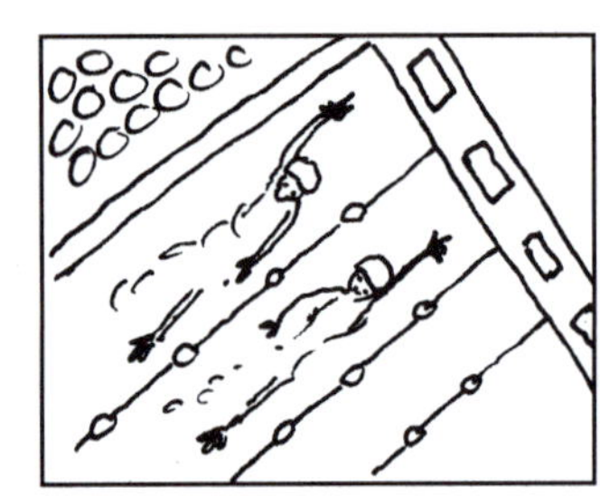

s c

l t

2 Circle the letter that makes the last sound.

t d

l t

p d

p g

m n

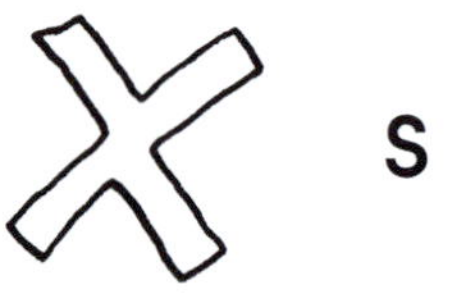

s c

3 Write a or i for the middle sound.

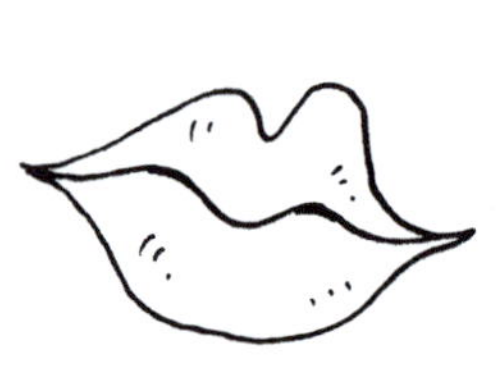

l _ ps

s _ d

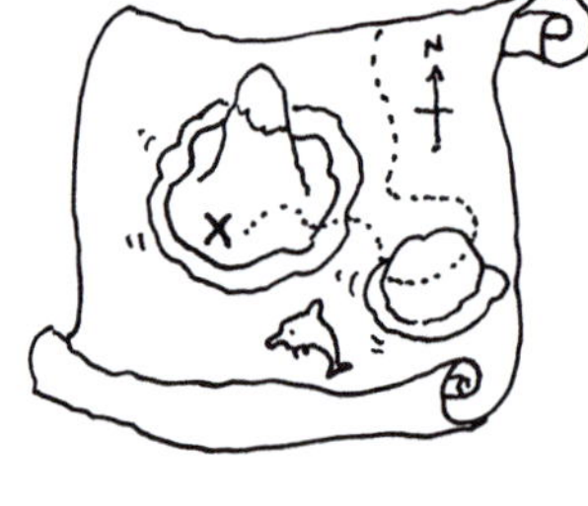

m _ p

t _ g

l _ d

4 Make words with different letters.

s		______	l		______
l	ag	______	n	ip	______
n		______	d		______
g		______	t		______

5 Colour the correct word.

I [am | an] glad to meet you.

Do [no | not] dig in the sand pit.

[Do | Did] Pam [do | did] her best?

Can I [go | got] to the park? Dad [as | is] looking for his cap there.

6 Write the word for more than one. Add **s**.

pig ______

mat ______

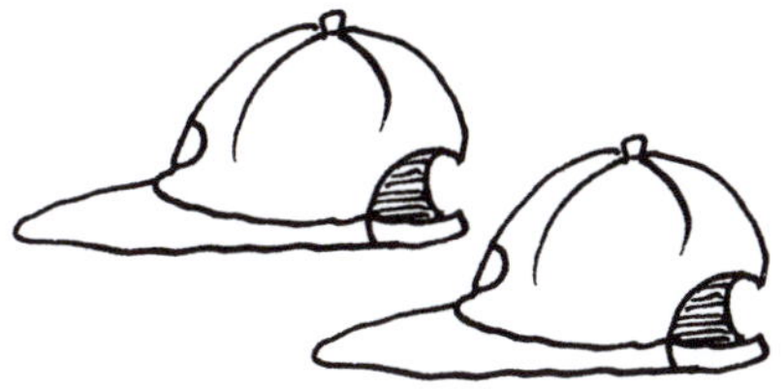

cap ______

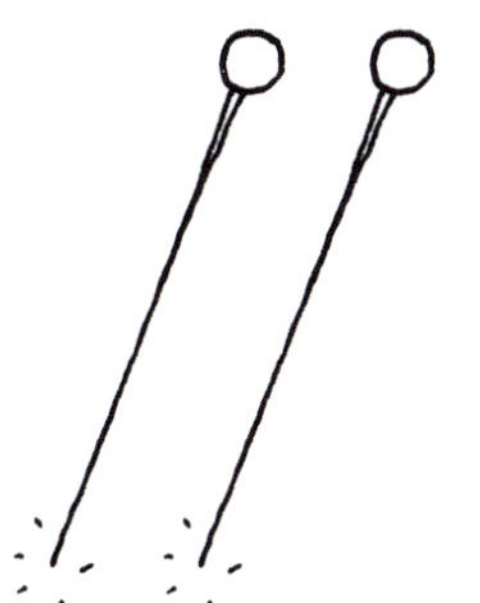

pin ______

Spelling Rules! Student Book K (ISBN 9780655092575)

Unit 8

Find a hidden o.

dog	not	got

log	pot	nod

dot	go	so

1 Say each word. Write the letter that makes the last sound.

2 Write a list word that rhymes.

pot _ _ _ pod _ _ _ no _ _

Spelling Rules! Student Book K (ISBN 9780655092575) © Janelle Ho, Helen Pearson/Matilda Education Australia

Make words with different last sounds.

no < d ____________

no < t ____________

Write words that match the pictures.

Do n_ _ pat

the d_ _.

D_ n_ _ put a hot

p_ _ o_ the table.

_ _ _ _ _ s_t

on the l_g.

My own words

____________ ____________ ____________

____________ ____________ ____________

Unit 9

bat	big	bin

rob	rip	rod

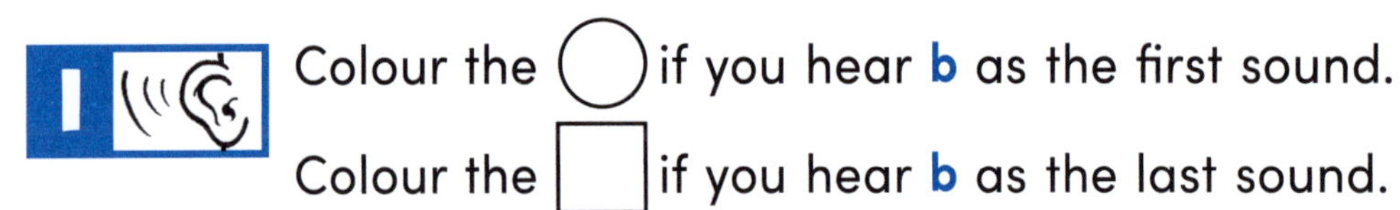

1 Colour the ◯ if you hear **b** as the first sound.
Colour the ☐ if you hear **b** as the last sound.

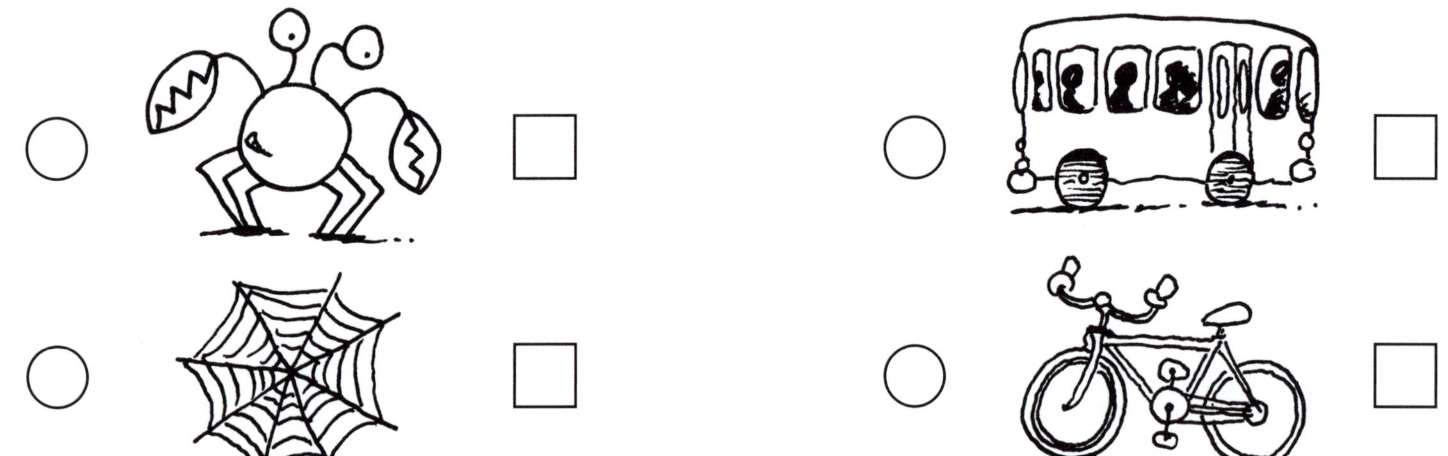

2 Change one letter to make a list word.

(n)od (t)in (s)ip (s)ob

_____ _____ _____ _____

3 Write the word for more than one.

2 ____________ 3 ____________ 4 ____________

4 Write words that rhyme.

pig

____

____

mat

____

____

rag

____

____

5 Write list words.

good ____________

small ____________

6 Write the list word.

An Aboriginal word that means 'family' ____________

My own words

____________ ____________ ____________

____________ ____________ ____________

Unit 10

Find a hidden **b**.

has	had	an

his	hot	egg

he	she	me

Put a ◯ around the words starting with **e**.

Put a ☐ around the words starting with **h**.

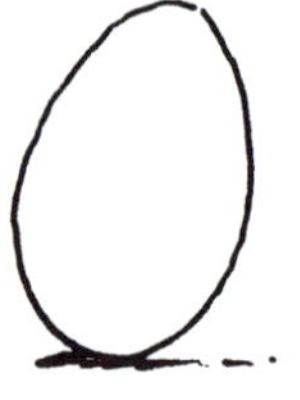

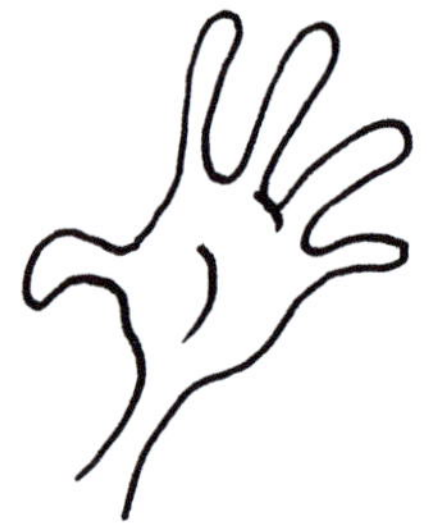

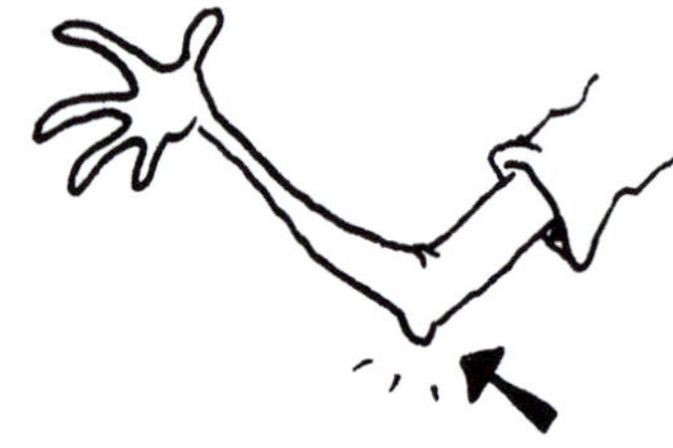

Make words with these letters.

____

____

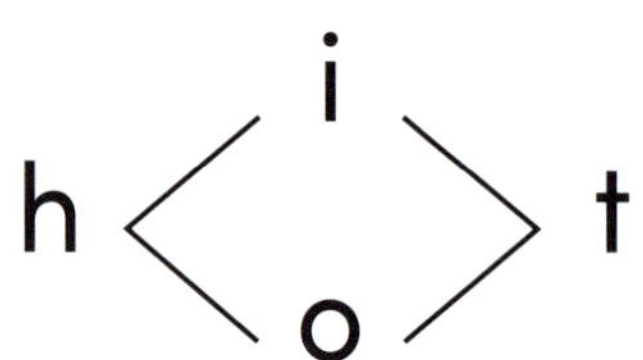

____

____

an goes before **a**, **e**, **i**, **o**, **u**.
a goes before other letters.

3 Write **a** or **an** for each picture.

______  ______  ______ 

______  ______  ______ 

4 Circle the letter that makes the first sound.

 e h n

 h e a

 e a h

5 Write list words.

When it is _ _ _, Pat wears _ _ _ hat.

Sal _ _ _ an _ _ _.  She gave it to _ _.

My own words

______ ______ ______

______ ______ ______

ten	red	bed

get	pet	step

him	my	by

1 Colour the shapes with e red.

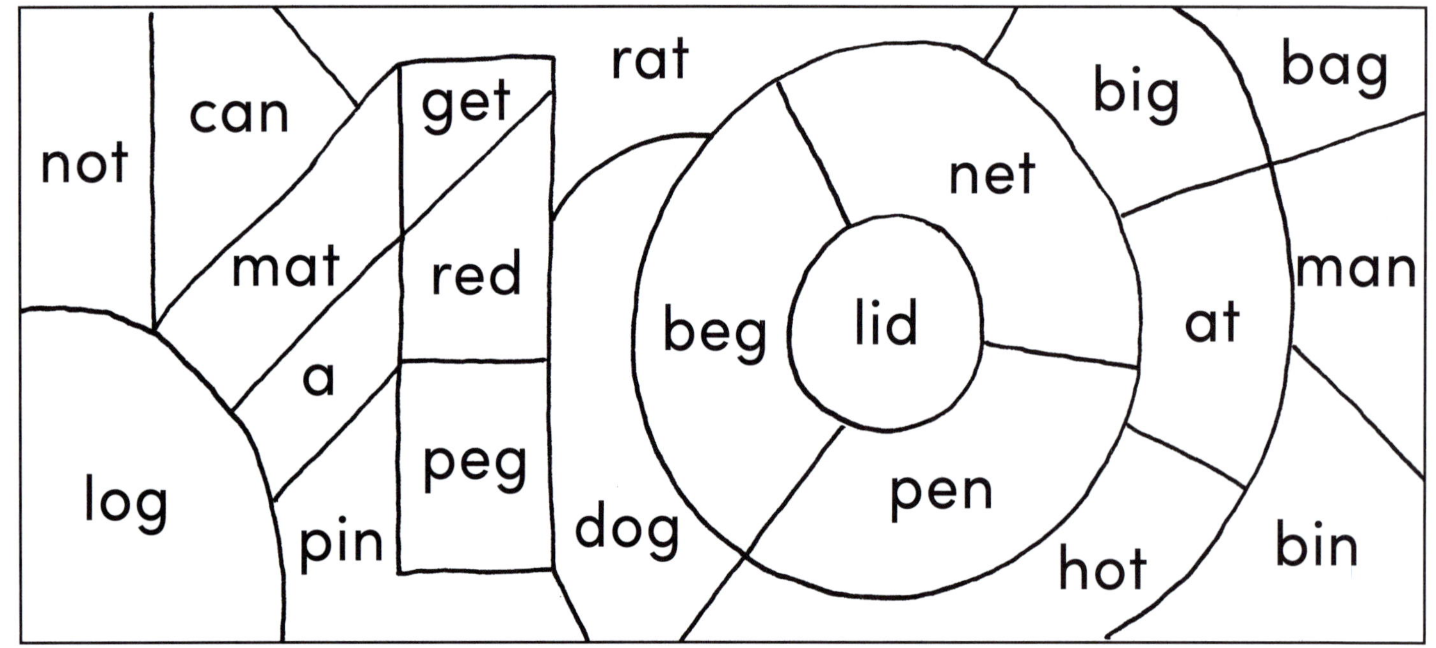

2 Write list words that rhyme.

pen ____________ set ____________ ____________

by ____________ led ____________ ____________

Spelling Rules! Student Book K (ISBN 9780655092575) © Janelle Ho, Helen Pearson/Matilda Education Australia

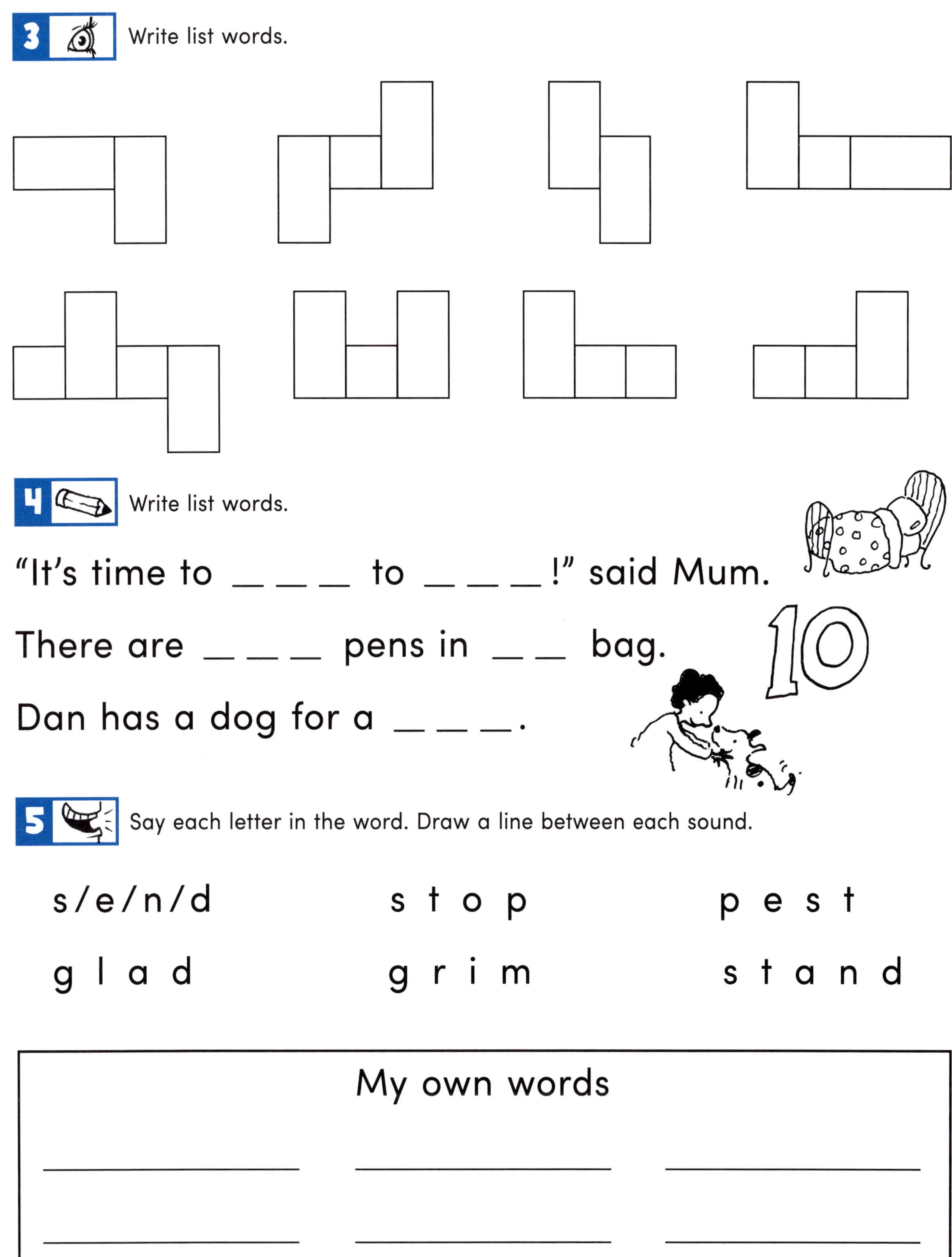

3 Write list words.

4 Write list words.

"It's time to _ _ _ to _ _ _ _!" said Mum.

There are _ _ _ pens in _ _ bag.

Dan has a dog for a _ _ _.

5 Say each letter in the word. Draw a line between each sound.

s/e/n/d s t o p p e s t

g l a d g r i m s t a n d

My own words

Unit 12

Find a hidden **u**.

fat	fan	fit

fog	up	us

or	one	fin

1 Draw something else that begins with the same sound.

f

u

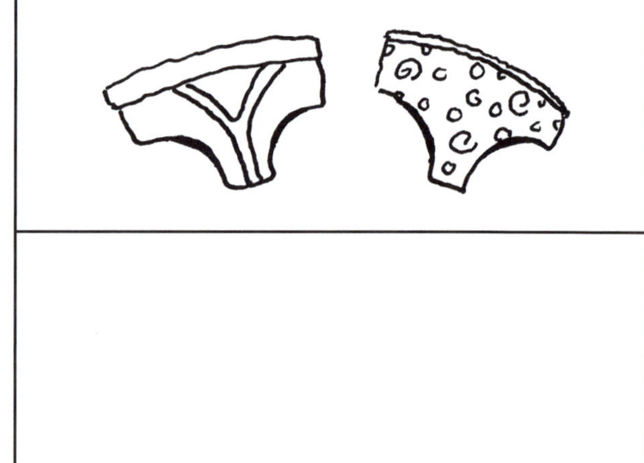

2 Write a list word that has the small word in it.

an ______ in ______ on ______ it ______

Spelling Rules! Student Book K (ISBN 9780655092575) © Janelle Ho, Helen Pearson/Matilda Education Australia

3 Write list words.

Ron has ☐☐☐ ☐☐☐ cat.

My fish has a red ☐☐☐.

"Wake ☐☐!" Rita's mother said.

4 Write **he** or **she** and a list word.

My uncle says _ _ wants to give _ _ a dog.

Ann says _ _ _ wants a pig _ _ a dingo.

5 Write list words.

down ________ ________ thin

My own words

________ ________ ________

________ ________ ________

Unit 13

Find a hidden f.

of	if	puff

mum	sun	bus

off	hug	put

1 Write the letter that makes the last sound.

 ____

 ____

 ____

2 Write **of**.

a cup _ _ nuts

a jar _ _ jam

Spelling Rules! Student Book K (ISBN 9780655092575) © Janelle Ho, Helen Pearson/Matilda Education Australia

3 Write **if** and a list word.

I will _ _ _ _ on my cap _ _ it is hot.

The _ _ _ _ will stop for me _ _ I wave.

Do not mix up **of** and **off**. *one **of** us* *turn it **off***

4 Write **of** or **off**.

Get _____ the bus at the last stop.

One _____ my eggs is still hot.

My own words		
______________	______________	______________
______________	______________	______________

Spelling Rules! Student Book K (ISBN 9780655092575) © Janelle Ho, Helen Pearson/Matilda Education Australia

Unit 14

Find a hidden j.

jam	jog	kid

be	we	the

to	just	are

1 Say the words. Cross out pictures that do not start with j.

2 Say the words. Cross out pictures that do not start with k.

3 Write list words.

4 Write list words.

5 Write **j** or **k** for the first sound.

______ ______ ______

6 Circle the pairs of words that rhyme.

job	so
be	go
we	are

My own words

______ ______ ______

______ ______ ______

Write the letter that makes the first sound. Cross out the picture that does not belong.

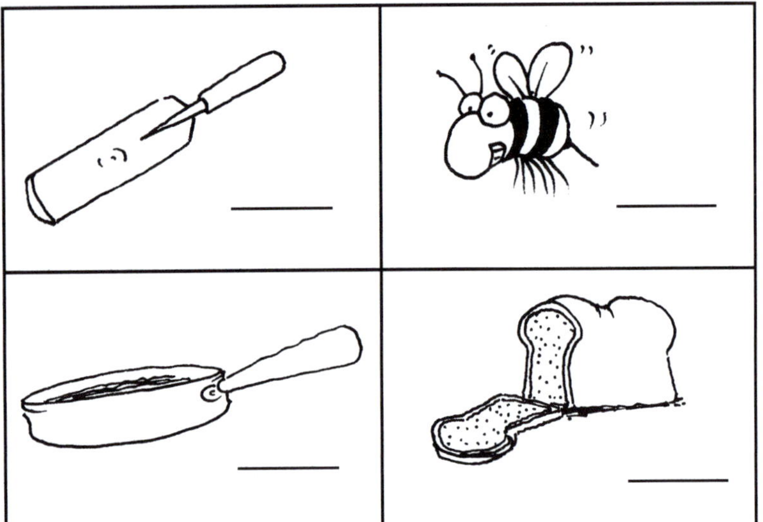

Write a pair of words.

I will ____________

and __________ and

blow the house

down.

Spelling Rules! Student Book K (ISBN 9780655092575) © Janelle Ho, Helen Pearson/Matilda Education Australia

Say each word. Write the letter to finish the word.

_an 

h_g 

j_m 

be_ 

_od 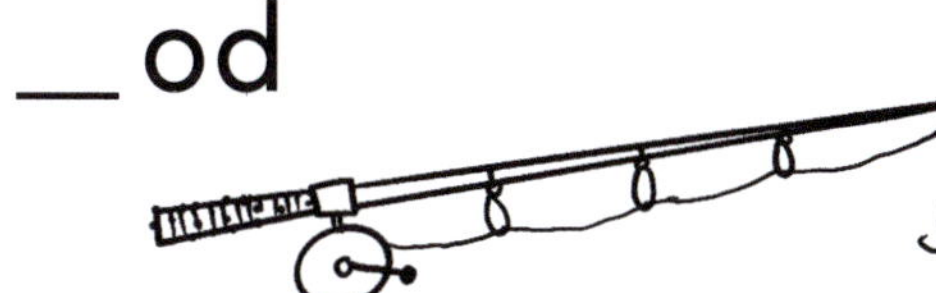

t_n 

Write **a** or **an**.

_____ 

_____ 

_____ 

_____ 

_____  

_____ 

Write **can** if you can do each thing.

I _______ read a book.

I _______ hit a ball.

I _______ draw a cat.

Write a word for each clue.

not good = ___________

not bottom = ___________

not cold = ___________

not yes = ___________

not on = ___________

not down = ___________

Unit 16

Find a hidden **and**.

and	but	too

out	for	her

our	said	you

1 Make words with these letters.

h b r	e u	t g b

j	o u	g

e a	nd

2 Write two list words that rhyme.

3 Write list words.

"Mum _ _ _ _ I must get _ _ _ an egg.

Will _ _ _ help me?"

Write a word from the box.

and	A rat is big, ________ a pig is bigger.
if	Sip a drink ________ you are hot.
but	Gus has a bat ________ a ball in his bag.

Do not mix up **to** and **too**.

*have **to** go* *next **to** me*

*run **too** fast* *pots and pans **too***

Write **to** or **too**.

Her bag is _____ big _____ fit in the car.

Ten pets are _____ many for us.

My own words

______________ ______________ ______________

______________ ______________ ______________

Unit 17

Find a hidden **z**.

van	wet	web

yes	zip	zoo

yet	was	will

1 Draw a line to join pictures that start with the same sound.

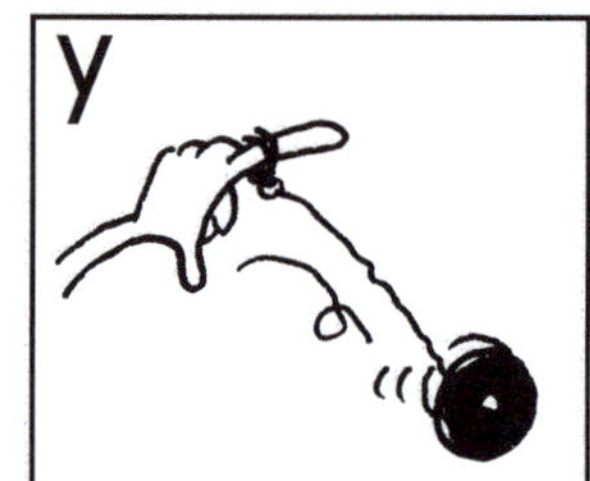

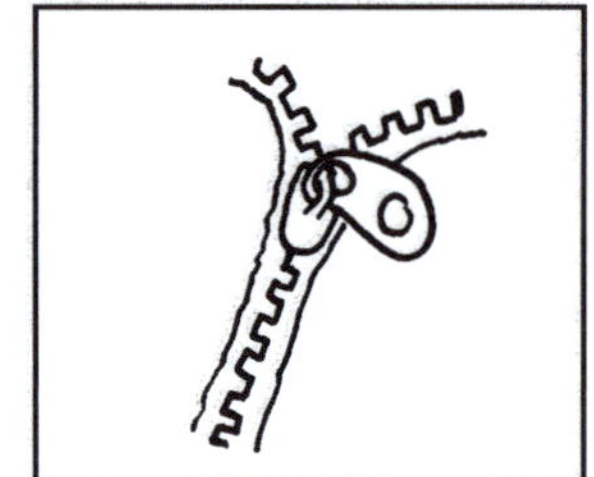

2 Circle the words you see.

y z o o q v a n t n o f z w e t o y e s q u w a s

Spelling Rules! Student Book K (ISBN 9780655092575) © Janelle Ho, Helen Pearson/Matilda Education Australia

3 Write list words that rhyme.

Jan's dog has a ________ nose.

Gran has not had her nap ________ .

4 Write **was** or **will**.

________ you go for a jog?

Zac's old van ________ red.

5 Answer the questions. Write **Yes, I do.** or **No, I don't.**

Do you play the violin? ________________________

Do you have a yo-yo? ________________________

6 Finish the question. Use as many list words as you can. Then write an answer.

_______ _______ like ________?

____

My own words

________ ________ ________

________ ________ ________

Unit 18

Find a hidden x.

six	mix	wax

box	fox	axe

went	very	school

1 Say the words. Write the first letter.

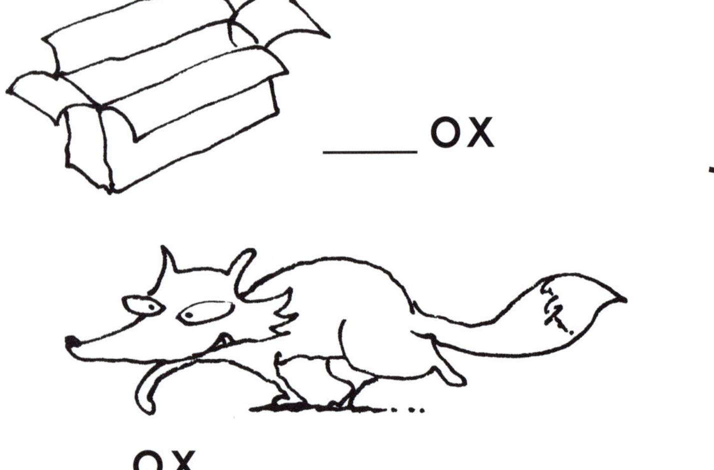

___ox

___ox

___ax

___ix

___ix

2 Write **go** or **went**.

I ________ to school by bus on Fridays.

Last week after school, I ________ to the park.

Write the words that rhyme on the same box.

wax mix fix box six fox tax axe

4 Write list words.

Max has ________ socks.

He puts his socks in a ________.

If you ________ yellow and blue paint, you get green.

I am at ______________ by 8.30 am.

5 Finish the sentence.

My school is called ____________________________________.

My own words

Unit 19

Find a hidden zz.

miss	less	fuss

hiss	loss	buzz

mess	fizz	class

1 Write a list word that rhymes.

less miss toss bus

_______ _______ _______ _______

2 Find the ss words in the word worm. Write them on the lines.

_______ _______ _______

_______ _______ _______

Spelling Rules! Student Book K (ISBN 9780655092575) © Janelle Ho, Helen Pearson/Matilda Education Australia

3 Make words with these letters.

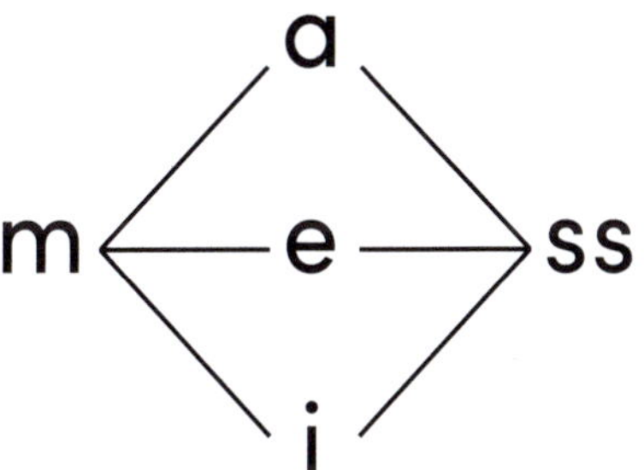

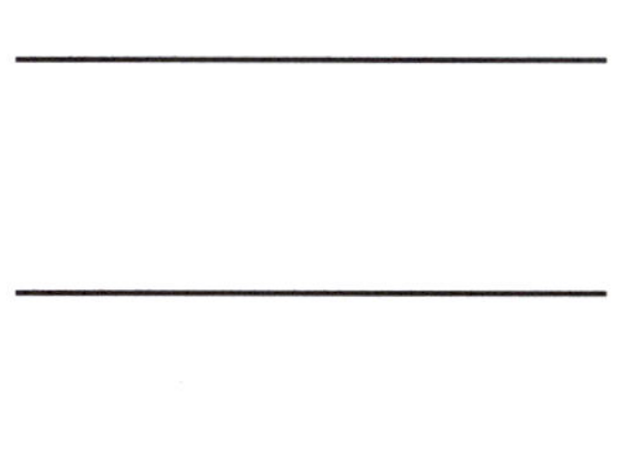

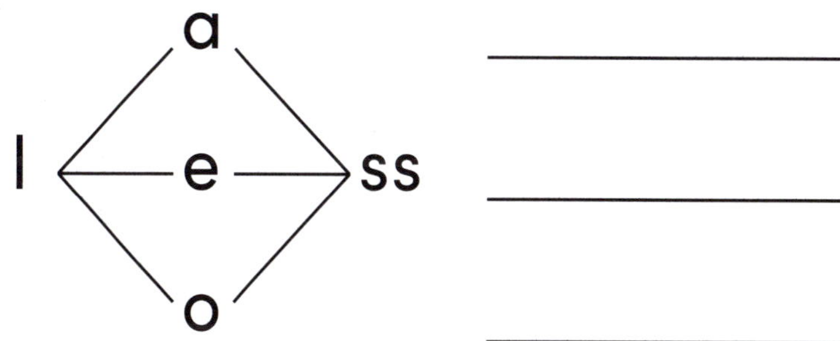

ss and **zz** do not start a word.

4 Write **s**, **ss**, **z** or **zz**.

bu____

____oo

____it

fi____

mi____

My own words

______________ ______________ ______________

______________ ______________ ______________

Spelling Rules! Student Book K (ISBN 9780655092575)

Unit 20

Find a hidden **y**.

fry	fly	why

try	cry	sky

this	that	boy

1 Write list words.

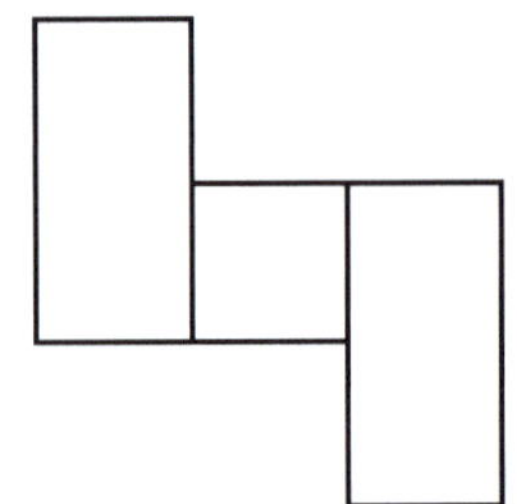

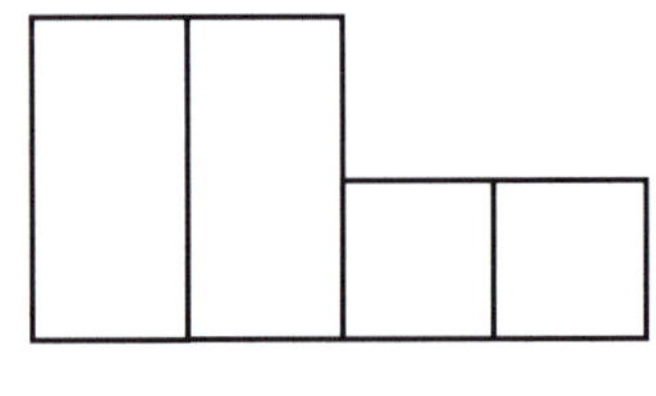

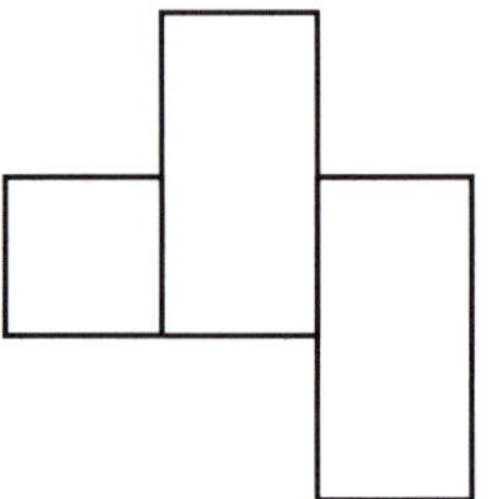

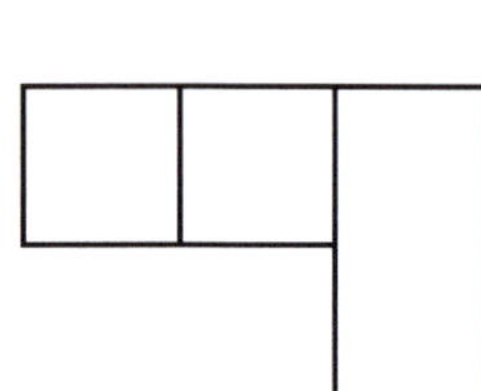

2 Change one letter to make a list word.

s (t) y

______ ______ ______

3 Write a list word.

Question: ________ are dogs like trees?

Answer: They both have barks!

Spelling Rules! Student Book K (ISBN 9780655092575) © Janelle Ho, Helen Pearson/Matilda Education Australia

4 What are these people saying? Write list words.

Don't ______.

How do birds ______?

A _____ left _____ bag.

Tip

by, **bye** and **buy** all sound the same.

***by** myself* ***bye-bye**!* ***buy** a gift*

5 Write **by**, **bye** or **buy**.

Mum will be home ______ dinner.

I have to ______ a new bed.

Wes said a loud "______!" as he left.

My own words

______ ______ ______

______ ______ ______

Unit 21

lots	any	many

some	two	how

1 Circle the right word.

bag bags

hen hens

2 Write to show more than one. Add s.

2 ________

3 ________

4 ________

2 ________

3 Circle the right word.

Tim does not have | any | lots | pets.

Dad puts | lots | many | of jam on his toast.

Mum drinks | any | many | cups of tea.

4 Write **how** and **many**. Then write an answer.

How ________ eggs are in the pan?

There are ________ ________.

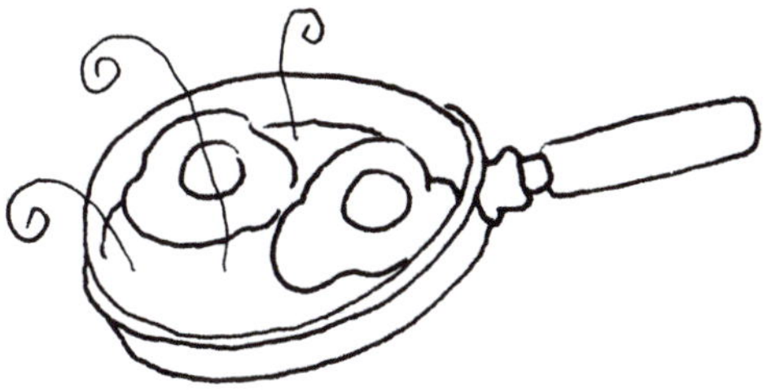

________ ________ cups are there?

There are ________ ________.

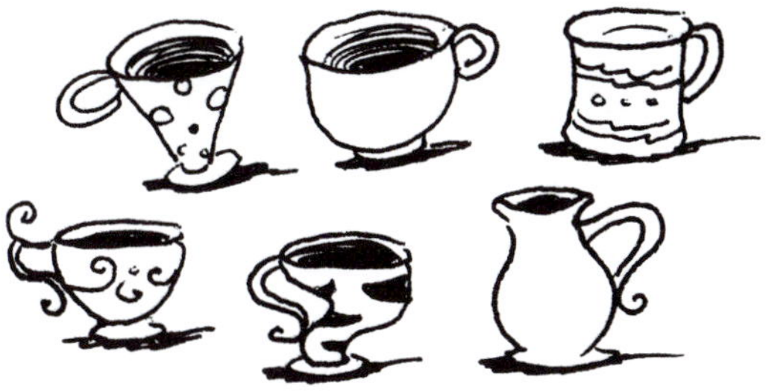

________ many cats are on the mat?

There are ________ ________.

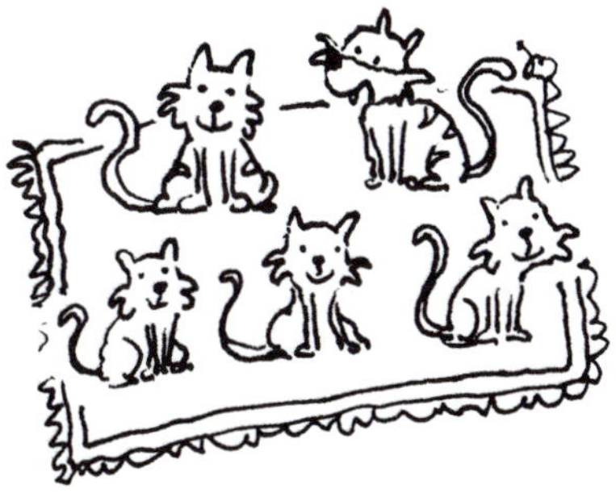

5 Circle the wrong word. Write the correct one.

Jon has too school caps. ____________

6 Write a sentence using the word in the box.

some	______________________________
many	______________________________

My own words

________ ________ ________

________ ________ ________

Unit 22 Revision

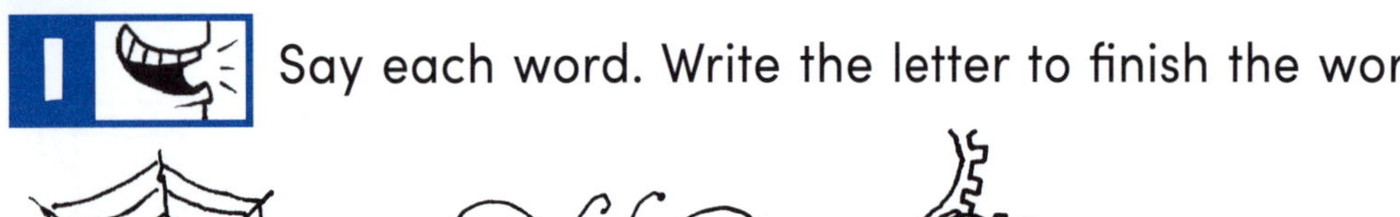

1 Say each word. Write the letter to finish the word.

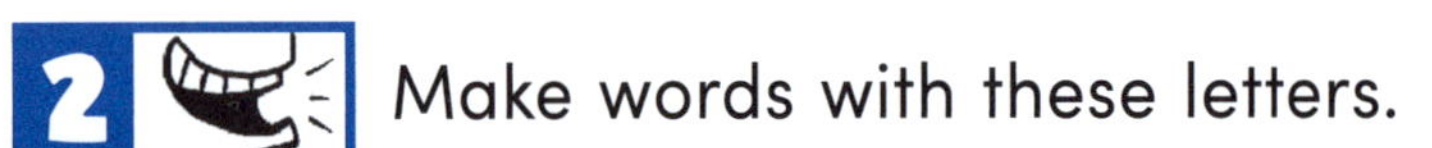

2 Make words with these letters.

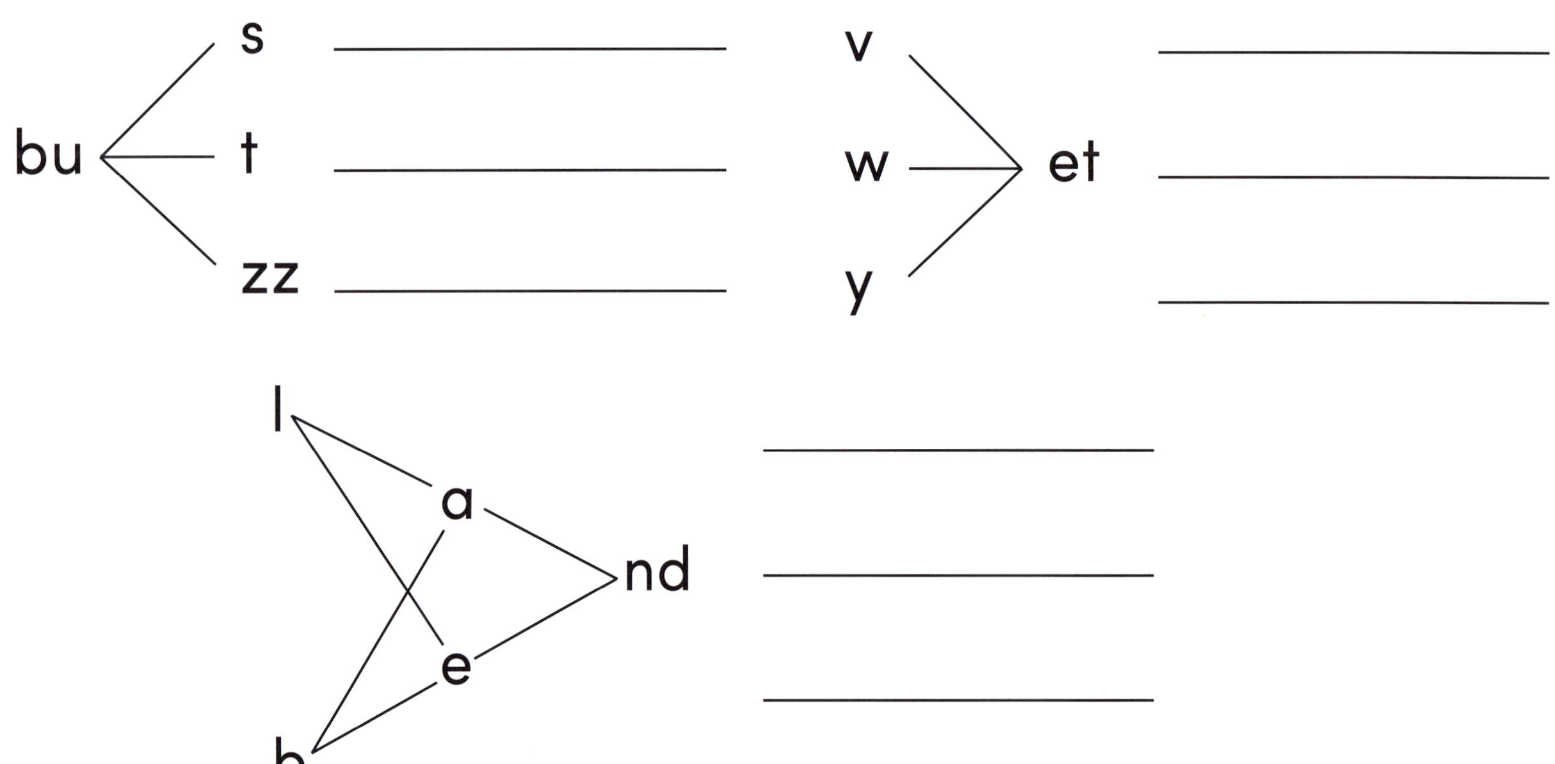

3 Circle the words you see.

Spelling Rules! Student Book K (ISBN 9780655092575) © Janelle Ho, Helen Pearson/Matilda Education Australia

4 Write the letters to finish the word.

bees bu __ __   snakes hi __ __   drinks fi __ __

5 Colour the correct word.

It is to | too late to go out | our!

Max has some | lots salt on his chips.

How any | many eggs are there?

We only have to | too | two. We must by | buy | bye more.

6 Write the correct word.

and / but	
	Tom likes butter ________ jam on his toast.
	Tim likes butter ________ no jam on his.

how / why	
	I know ________ to swim.
	I know ________ I learned to swim.

7 Why are these words wrong?

ssun   zzoo

____

Spelling Rules! Student Book K (ISBN 9780655092575) © Janelle Ho, Helen Pearson/Matilda Education Australia

Unit 23

shy	shut	shoe

push	fish	wash

want	have	your

1 Say each word. Circle in red if the word starts with **sh**. Circle in blue if the word ends in **sh**.

2 Draw boxes to show the shape of the word.

shy shut push shoe

3 Write a list word that has the small word in it. Then add your own word.

is ______________ as ______________ us ______________

______________ ______________ ______________

Spelling Rules! Student Book K (ISBN 9780655092575) © Janelle Ho, Helen Pearson/Matilda Education Australia

4 Write list words.

I do not ____________ to go to the shop.

I ____________ to wash my hands.

Shut ____________ eyes and make a wish.

Shan has lost his left ____________.

We have a pet ____________.

5 Write list words.

not open	not pull	not bold
____________	____________	____________

6 It is your birthday. Write what you wish for.

____

____

My own words

____________	____________	____________
____________	____________	____________

Spelling Rules! Student Book K (ISBN 9780655092575) © Janelle Ho, Helen Pearson/Matilda Education Australia

Unit 24

My children are still tadpoles.

chin	chat	chips

rich	much	such

chess	which	children

1 Colour **ch** words green. Colour **sh** words yellow.

2 Say both words. Colour the correct one.

I like eating fish and | ships | chips |.

My bike helmet has a clip under my | shin | chin |.

I lost my bag at the | shops | chops |.

Spelling Rules! Student Book K (ISBN 9780655092575) © Janelle Ho, Helen Pearson/Matilda Education Australia

3 Write list words.

__________ jam do you like best?

Her bark is __________ worse than her bite.

Nish's room is __________ a mess!

Rule

Most words add **s** to show there is more than one.

Some words change:

man → men *child → children*

Some words stay the same:

sheep *deer* *fish*

4 Write the word that shows more than one.

one book, two __________ one child, two __________

one foot, two __________ one nose, two __________

one man, two __________ one sheep, two __________

My own words

__________ __________ __________

__________ __________ __________

Spelling Rules! Student Book K (ISBN 9780655092575) © Janelle Ho, Helen Pearson/Matilda Education Australia

Unit 25

Find a hidden **ck**.

back	duck	neck

sick	sock	shock

were	does	what

1 Write the middle sound.

d __ ck

n __ ck

sh __ ck

2  Make words with different first sounds.

r / sh / l → ock ______ ______ ______

b / p / s → ack ______ ______ ______

3 Write list words.

I do not feel well. I am ________.

Dad ________ not like his new red and black ________s.

Guess ________ happened

when the dog ate a clock?

It got a lot of ticks.

Most words add **ed** to show an action happened in the past.

shock → *shocked* *push* → *pushed*

4 Add **ed** to show the past tense.

Bess duck__ __ so she did not get hit.

Grandpa wish__ __ that he had not rush__ __.

I kiss__ __ Mum goodbye before I left.

My own words

________ ________ ________

________ ________ ________

Unit 26

Find a hidden ll.

hill	shall	doll

bell	fell	yell

all	call	full

1 Write list words.

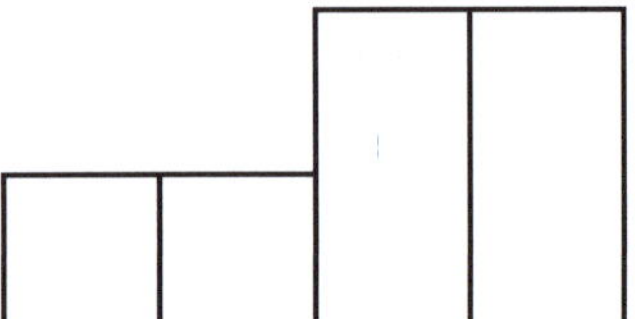

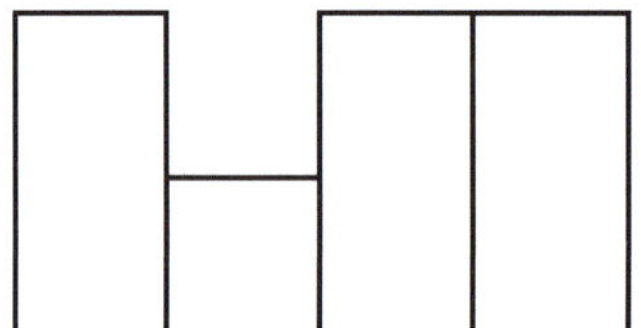

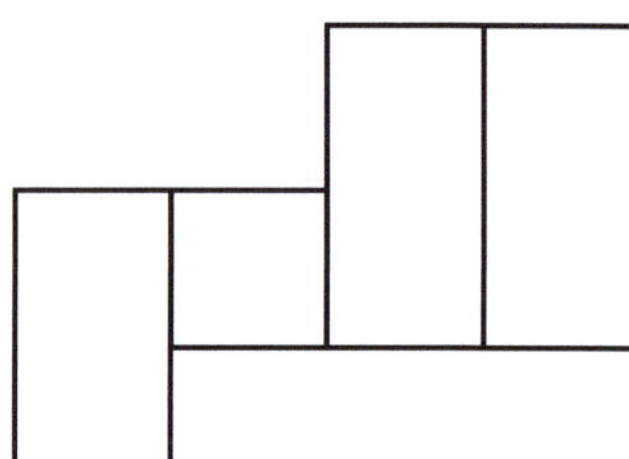

2 Write list words.

Ding, dong, ________ ,

Pussy's in the well!

Jack and Jill went up the ________

to fetch a pail of water.

Say each word. Circle the word that does not rhyme.

all call shall fall

Say the words. Circle the correct word.

Mum | shall | shell | take me to the beach on Sunday.

I like games that let us | bell | yell | loudly.

Bill ate so much that he is | full | fell |.

English words do not begin with double consonants.
The word *llama* is from South America.

Circle all the words that are wrong.

The zzip on my bbag is bbroken. Mum llooked at it and ssaid she would ffix it. She asked me to ssit with her as she ddid it.

My own words

__________ __________ __________

__________ __________ __________

Unit 27

then	them	they

thick	with	both

three	four	when

1 Colour 1 if **th** is the first sound.
Colour 2 if **th** is a middle sound.
Colour 3 if **th** is the last sound.

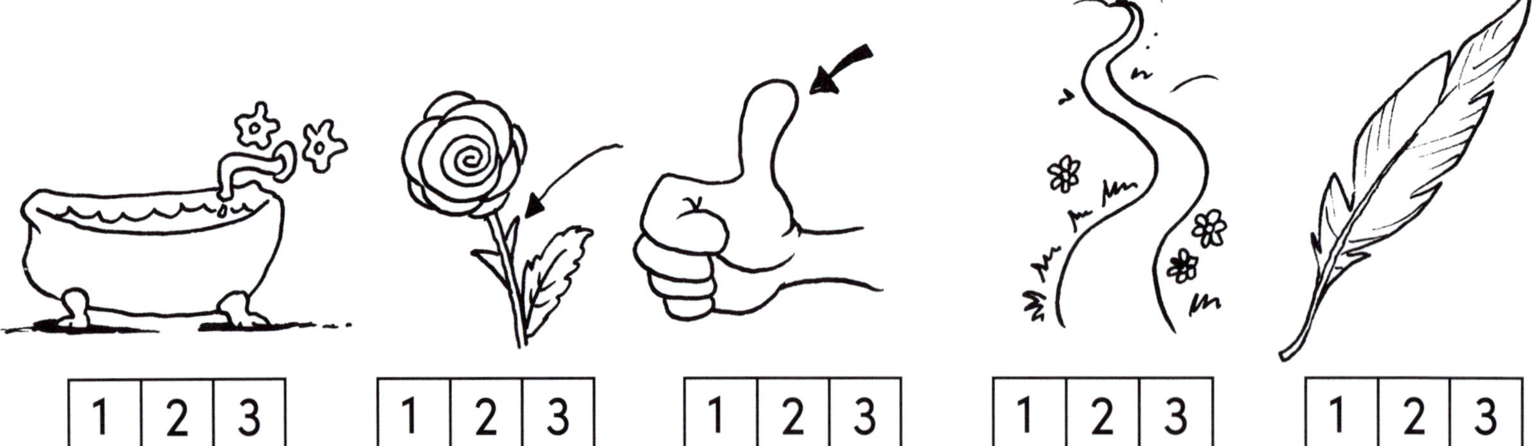

1	2	3		1	2	3		1	2	3		1	2	3		1	2	3

2 The vowels **a**, **i** or **o** have been left out of these words. Write the words with the missing vowel.

bth ________ mth ________ bth ________

pth ________ wth ________ thck ________

Spelling Rules! Student Book K (ISBN 9780655092575) © Janelle Ho, Helen Pearson/Matilda Education Australia

3 Write list words.

I went to the park. ________ I went to the shops.

________ does school end? It ends at 3 o'clock.

The children are having fun. Look at ________.

One, two, ________, ________.

4 Write **They**, **She** or **He**.

This is Tim. ________ is six.

I see Amit and Lil. ________ have good seats.

Nina is over there. ________ looks ill.

Look at Tess and Finn. ________ can run so fast!

5 Make a new word by adding **t** or **th** at the beginning.

hat ________ hen ________ is ________

here ________ in ________ his ________

My own words

________ ________ ________

________ ________ ________

Unit 28

sing	hang	long
sang	**hung**	**song**
bring	sting	thing

 Use the clues to make list words.

 ~~d~~ → g = ________

b +  = ________

 ~~i~~ → o = ________

 ~~w~~ → s = ________

 ~~l~~ → t = ________

 ~~k~~ → th = ________

 Say both words. Colour the correct one.

Monkeys like to | hung | hang | upside down.

We ran outside when the bell | rang | ring |.

Spelling Rules! Student Book K (ISBN 9780655092575) © Janelle Ho, Helen Pearson/Matilda Education Australia

You can add **ing** to many words:

jump → jumping   *look → looking*

Words ending in **ng** add **ing** too:

hang → hanging   *sing → singing*

Add **ing** to these words.

play ____________   grow ____________

shock ____________   go ____________

spell ____________   bring ____________

sting ____________   hang ____________

4 Make compound words.

some / no / any / every → thing

____

____

____

____

My own words

____________ ____________ ____________

____________ ____________ ____________

Unit 29

quit	quiz	quick

quack	queen	squash

question	quiet	quite

Tip q always goes with u.

1 Draw boxes to show the shape of the word.

quiz quite quiet

2 Write a list word that rhymes.

hit ________

tick ________

wash ________

rack ________

Spelling Rules! Student Book K (ISBN 9780655092575) © Janelle Ho, Helen Pearson/Matilda Education Australia

3 Write list words.

not slow ____________ not loud ____________

Tip Do not mix up **quiet** and **quite**.
be ***quiet*** ***quite*** *full*

Shhhhhhhhh

4 Colour the correct word.

The class is | quiet | quite | because it is reading time.

The queen looks | quiet | quite | sad.

5 Write a sentence using the word in the box.

quite	____________________
quiet	____________________
question	____________________

My own words

____________ ____________ ____________

____________ ____________ ____________

1 Circle the last sound.

sh ch ck   sh ch ck   sh th ch   sh th ch

2 Say each word. Cross out the word that does not rhyme.

duck	fall	wash
sack	call	push
quack	shall	squash

3 Add two letters to make a word.

_ _ op   ba _ _   _ _ ick

_ _ op   ba _ _   _ _ ick

ba _ _

Spelling Rules! Student Book K (ISBN 9780655092575) © Janelle Ho, Helen Pearson/Matilda Education Australia

4 Colour the correct word.

Matt | boxed | boxing | his things and put them away.

Can you hear the bell | rings | ringed | ringing |?

Ash | pulled | pulling | her pin out and

| pushed | pushing | her hair off her face.

5 Write the words that match the pictures.

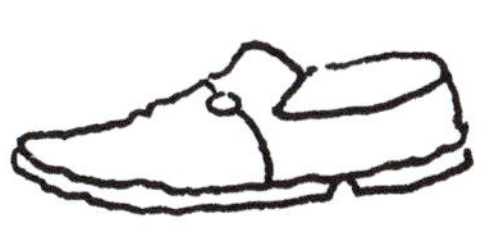  +  ________ and ________

  +  ________ and ________

 +  ________ and ________

6 Write the word.

  3 

one ________ ________ ________

Unit 31

My favourite game is leapfrog!

ate	name	take

safe	eve	these

shake	here	where

1 Circle the picture if you hear a long **a** sound.

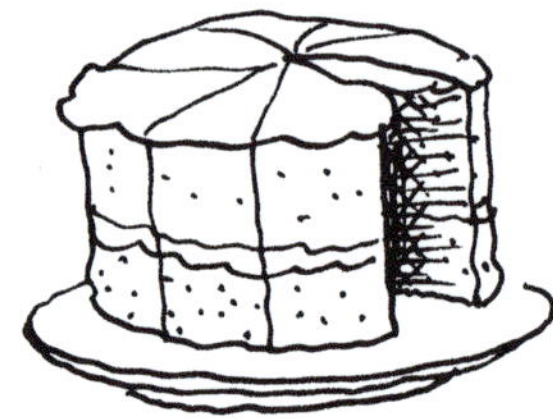

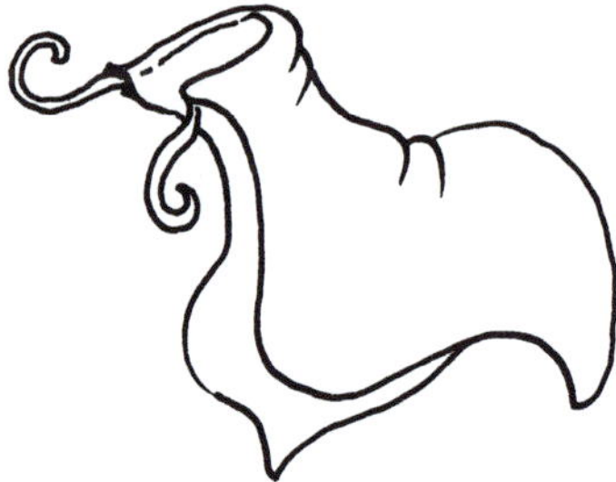

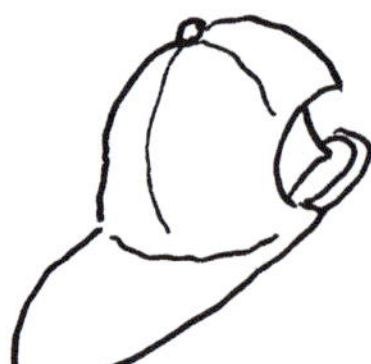
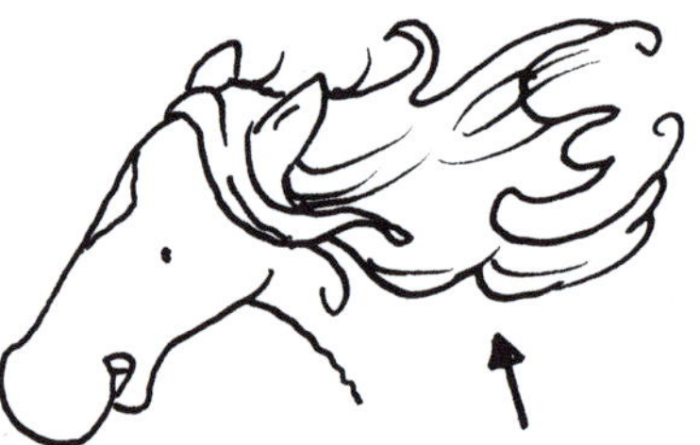

2 Circle all the **a–e** and **e–e** words in the word worm.

ateheremesamepaevecavepeastakemeat

Spelling Rules! Student Book K (ISBN 9780655092575) © Janelle Ho, Helen Pearson/Matilda Education Australia

3 Say both words. Colour the correct one.

I saw a lion | at | ate | the zoo.

I | hat | hate | wet days at school.

Don't walk on the | mat | mate | with muddy shoes.

4 Write list words.

I like the fireworks on New Year's ________.

________ is the best place to hide?

Come in ________ with me.

5 Use the letters in the word machine to make words. If you have more words, write them below.

sh g b l c t a k t m e

________ ________

________ ________

________ ________

________ ________ ________ ________ ________

My own words

________ ________ ________

________ ________ ________

Unit 32

like	smile	fine

hope	nose	rude

toe	June	those

1 Write the list words that have the same middle sound.

____

____

____

____

____

____

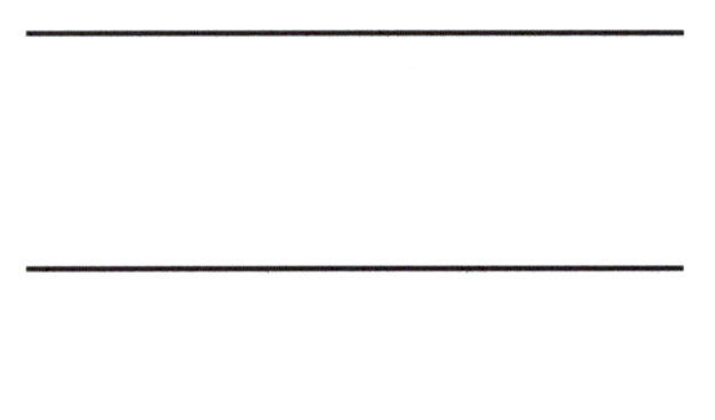

2 Write the missing vowels.

r __ ce 

sm __ le 

r __ pe 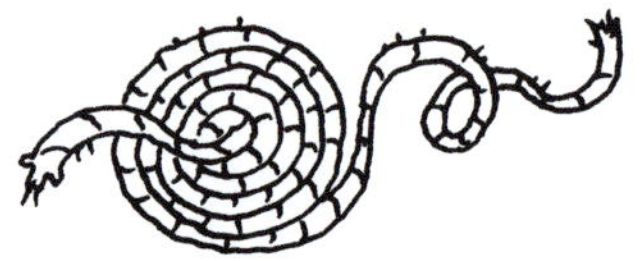

h __ se 

r __ de 

t __ ne

3 Look for a small word inside each word. Write the small word.

fine   nose   hope   toe

__________ __________ __________ __________

4 Colour the correct word.

Jill | like | likes | her new shoes.

We | hope | hopes | to finish the race.

| Smile | Smiles | at the camera!

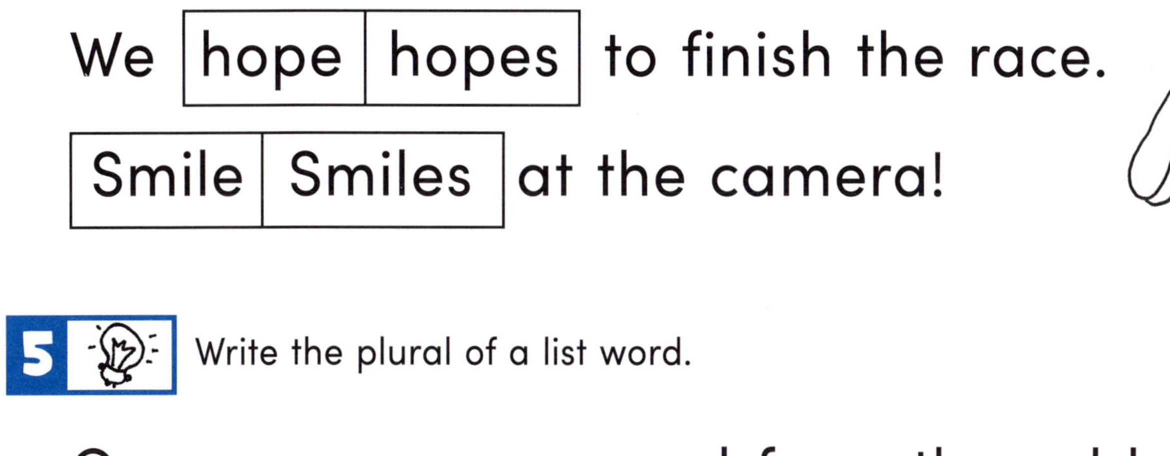

5 Write the plural of a list word.

Our __________ are red from the cold.

Our __________ are warm in our socks.

6 Write about something that happens in June.

____

____

My own words

__________ __________ __________

__________ __________ __________

Unit 33

see	bee	tree

feet	eat	ear

meat	each	clean

1 Write different words.

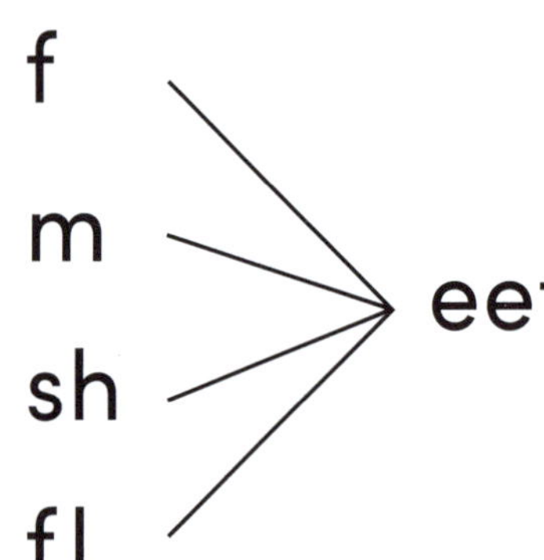

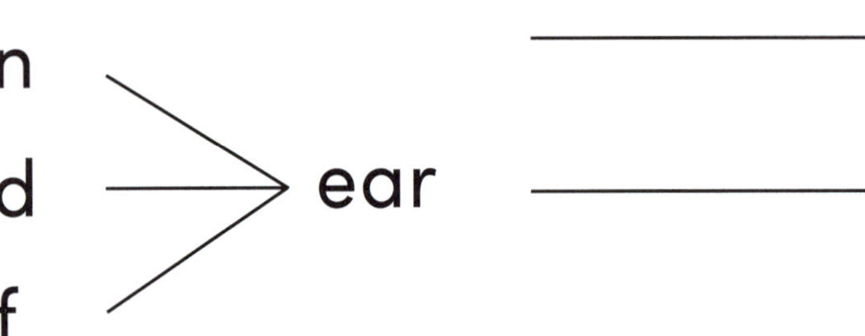

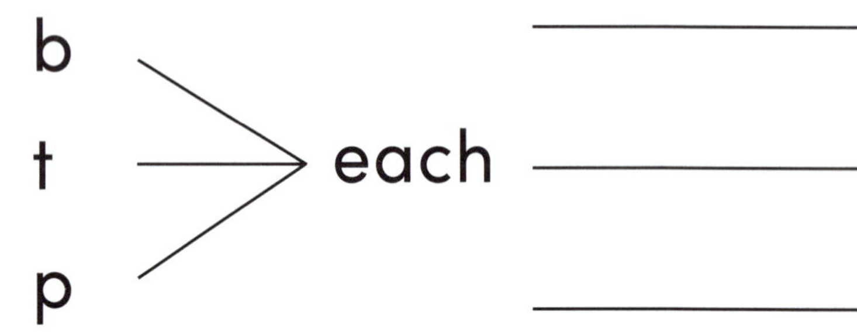

Look for **ee** words in the word worm. Colour each **ee** word green.

Some words sound the same, but are not spelt the same. *be bee sea see meat meet*

Colour the correct word.

I was stung by a | be | bee | while picking peas and beans.

Asha always | meets | meats | her friend at the bus stop.

Sharks live in the | see | sea |.

Write the plural word.

____________ ____________ ____________

My own words

____________ ____________ ____________

____________ ____________ ____________

Unit 34

boy	say	joy

boil	sail	join

play	plain	may

1 Write list words.

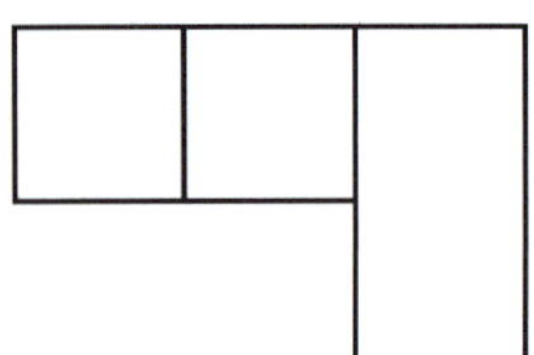
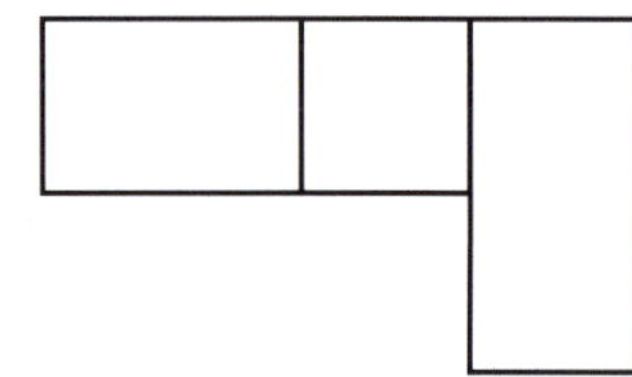
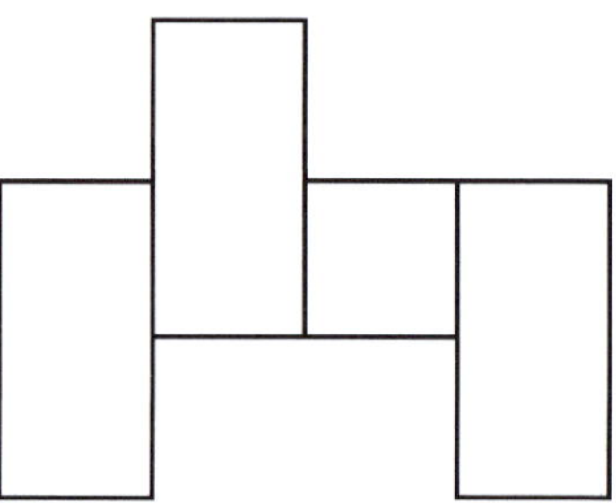
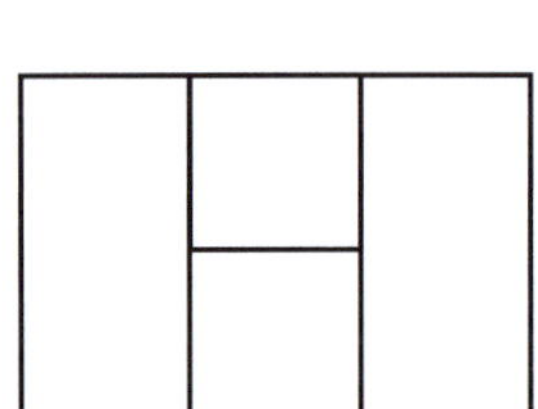
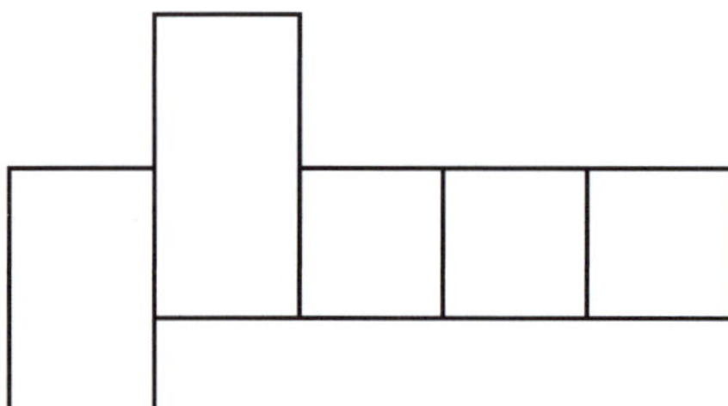
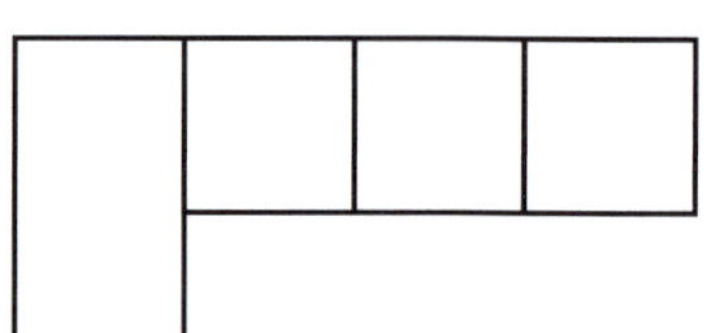

2 Write list words.

Spelling Rules! Student Book K (ISBN 9780655092575) © Janelle Ho, Helen Pearson/Matilda Education Australia

Change **oy** and **ay** to **oi** and **ai** when you add another consonant.

Use the Spelling Tip to make new words.

boy + l __________ joy + n __________

say + l __________ ray + n __________

may + l __________ stay + n __________

Write the words. Choose one to finish the sentence.

play — s __________
play — ed __________
play — ing __________

We __________ outside all day.

boil — s __________
boil — ed __________
boil — ing __________

Do not mess with __________ water.

My own words

__________ __________ __________

__________ __________ __________

Unit 35

My boat is slow!

how	down	slow

round	found	boat

row	grow	road

1 Use the letters to make words.

Use the letters to make new words. Write them under the word that rhymes.

Spelling Rules! Student Book K (ISBN 9780655092575) © Janelle Ho, Helen Pearson/Matilda Education Australia

Say **how**. Circle the words that have the same **ow** sound.

down blow growl round grow

3 Find a small word in the list word. Write the small word.

slow ____________ grow ____________

down ____________

Tip

The words **rode**, **rowed** and **road** are homophones. They have the same sound but are not spelt the same.

*Joan **rode** a horse, **rowed** a boat and then ran down the **road** to get home!*

4 Write **rode**, **rowed** or **road**.

Ning lives on the ____________ with jacaranda trees.

Eli ____________ the boat all by himself.

They ____________ their bikes at the park.

My own words

____________ ____________ ____________

____________ ____________ ____________

food	room	moon

grew	drew	flew

spoon	mood	chew

1 Write list words.

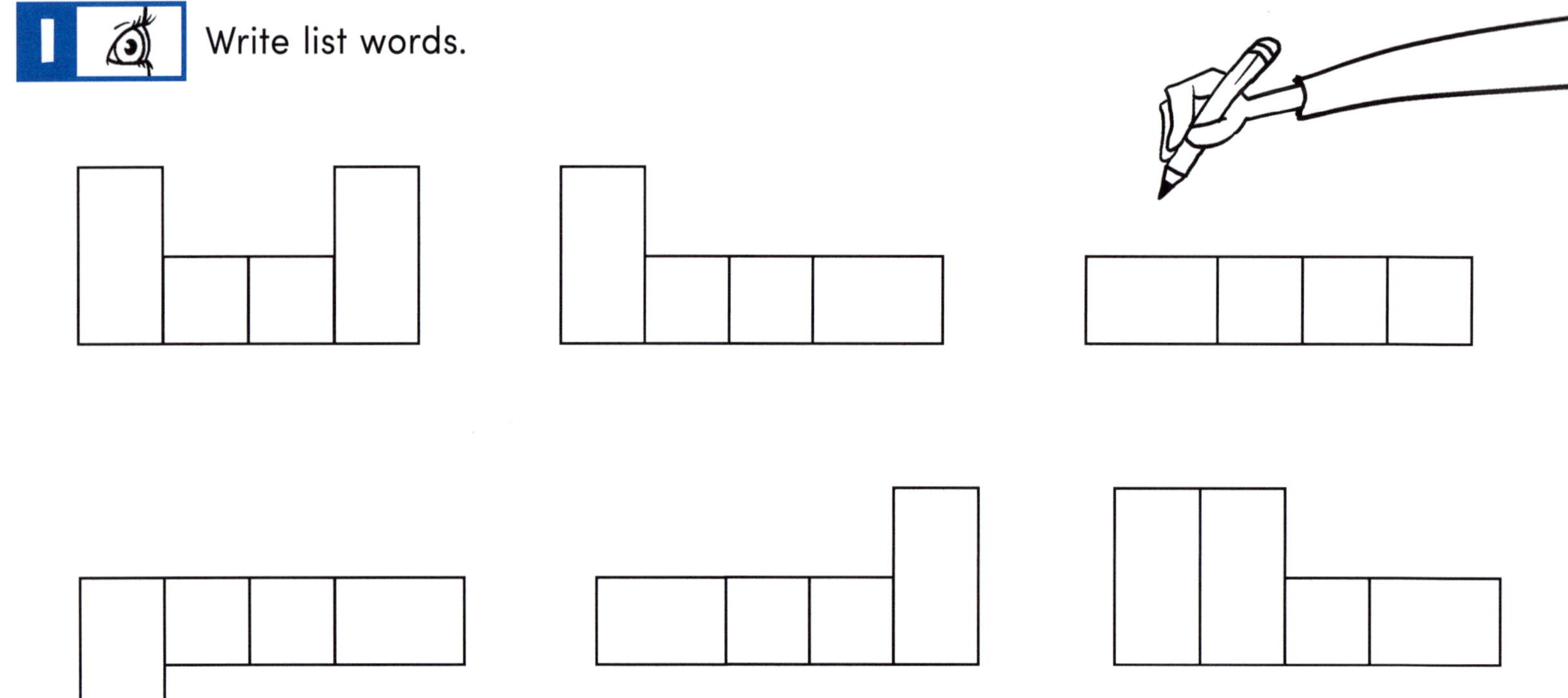

2 Say each word. Circle the words that have the same vowel sound as the list words.

fool book shoe toe four you

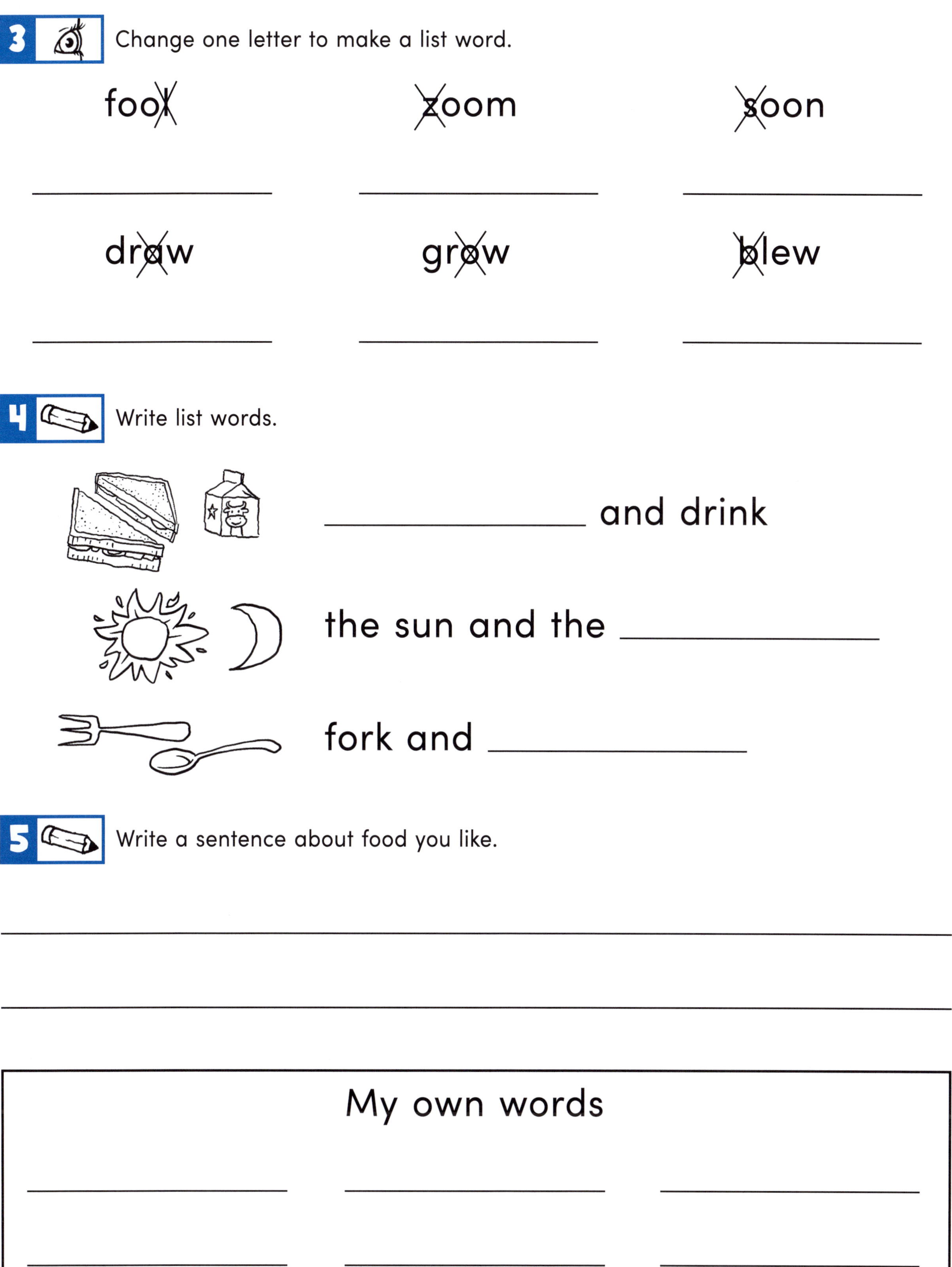

3 Change one letter to make a list word.

fool zoom soon

_______________ _______________ _______________

draw grow blew

_______________ _______________ _______________

4 Write list words.

_______________ and drink

the sun and the _______________

fork and _______________

5 Write a sentence about food you like.

____

____

My own words

_______________ _______________ _______________

_______________ _______________ _______________

Unit
37
Revision

Find the hidden a, e, i, o and u.

1 Write a word that fits the shape.

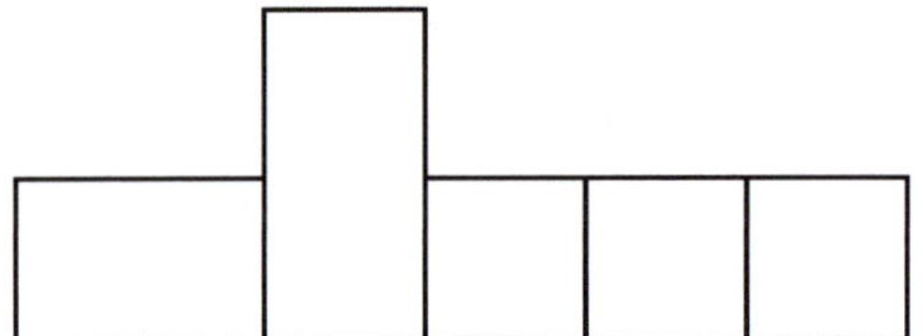
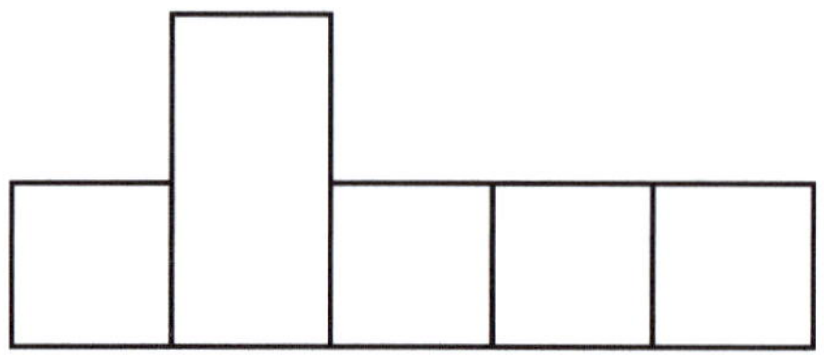
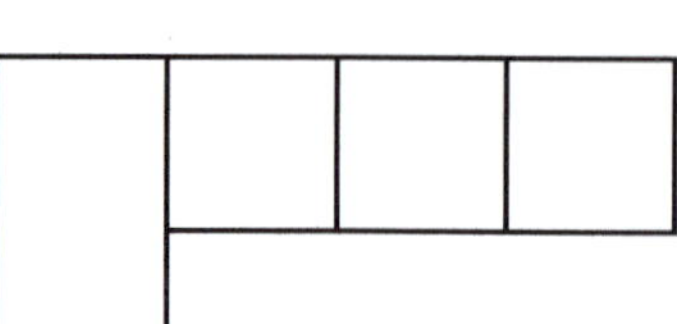
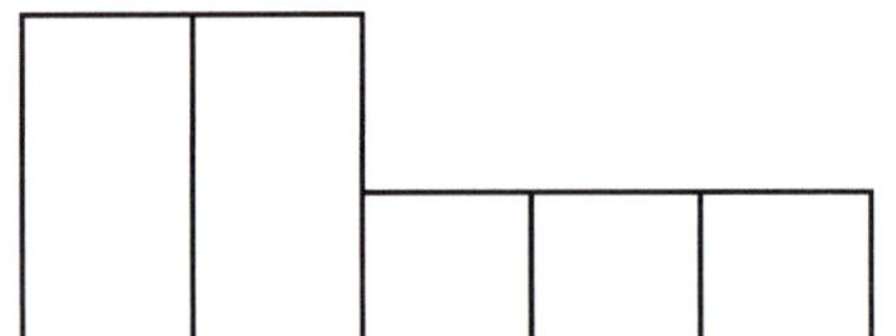
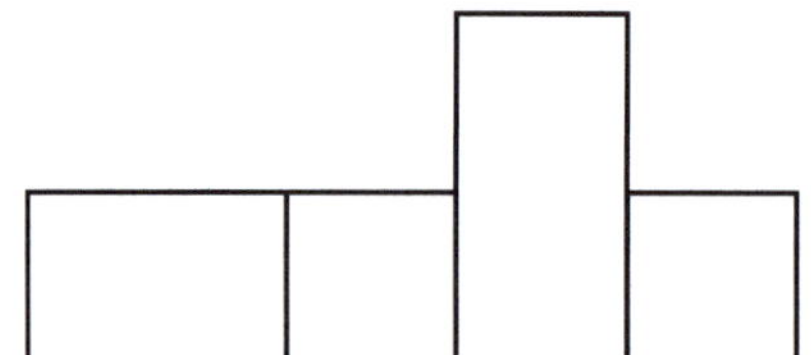
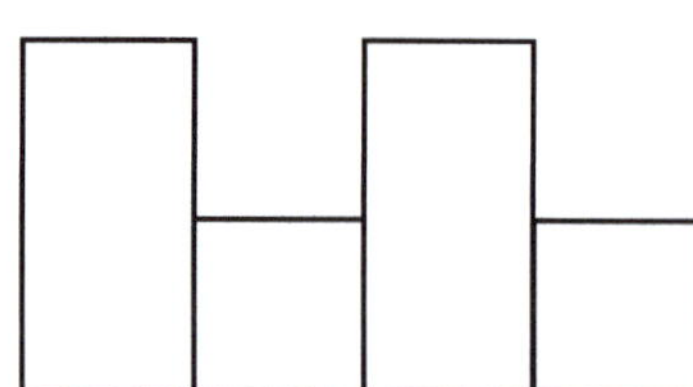

2 Use the clue to make new words.

pa~~t~~ + l = ______________

g + row + l = ______________

st + ring = ______________

pe~~g~~ + n = ______________

s + how + n = ______________

pl + at + e = ______________

Write one of your own. ______________________________________

3 Write the word. Match the body part to its use.

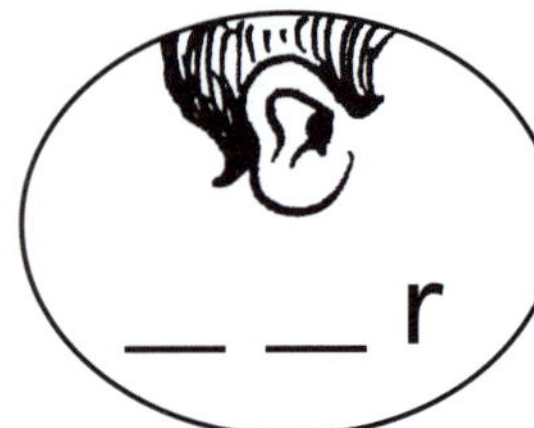

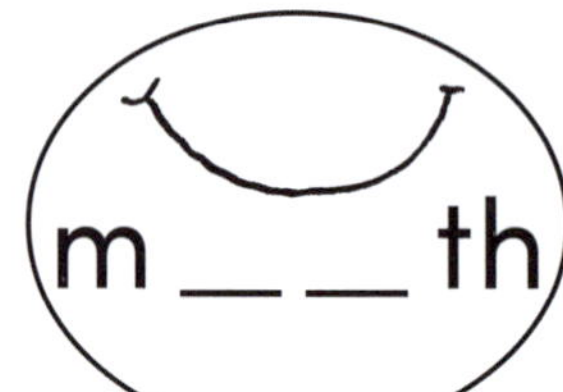

smell

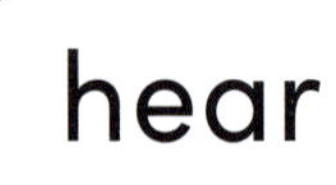

hear

feel

see

taste

4 Write the words. Choose one to finish the sentence.

join — s ________ | ed ________ | ing ________

She is ________ a new team soon.

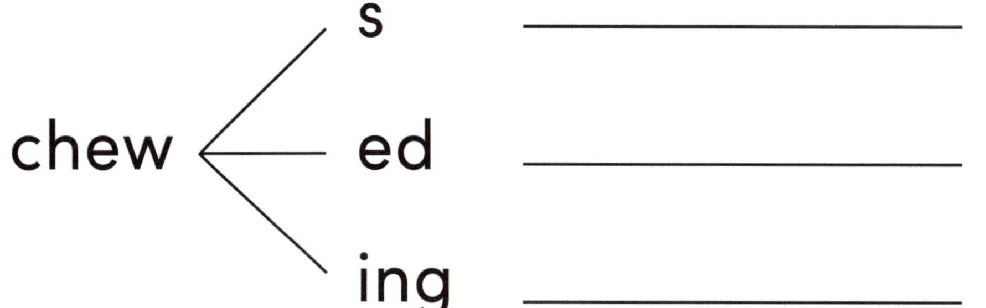

Yuri always ________ his food ten times.

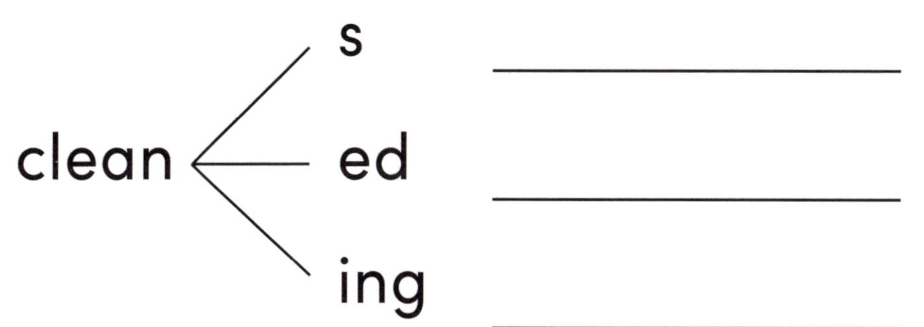

Lina ________ her shoes this morning.

Circle the mistake. Write the word correctly at the end.

Will you be seaing Rose at the game? ________

Yes, I will meat her at her home first. ________

I ate tree apples today. ________

Dad ran down the rode to get the bus. ________

Be quite. I want to read a book. ________

Take of your shoes at the door. ________

Unit
38

Find the **A** and the **a** in the bowl of alphabet soup.

Trace the letters. Write the same letter in lower case.

A ___	B ___	C ___	D ___	E ___
F ___	G ___	H ___	I ___	J ___
K ___	L ___	M ___	N ___	O ___
P ___	Q ___	R ___	S ___	T ___

U ___	V ___	W ___	X ___	Y ___	Z ___

2 Write the missing letters.

a ___ c d ___ f g ___ i j ___ l m n o ___ q r ___ t u ___ w ___ y z

___ B C ___ E F ___ H I ___ K L ___ N ___ P ___ ___ S T ___ V

___ X Y ___

 Answer each question.

What letter comes after b? ________

What letter comes after h? ________

What letter comes after n? ________

What letter comes after v? ________

 Finish each sentence.

My name is ____________________________________.

My teacher's name is ____________________________________.

My friend's name is ____________________________________.

My principal's name is ____________________________________.

 Finish each sentence.

The first letter of the alphabet is _____.

The last letter of the alphabet is _____.

List Words in Unit Order

Unit 2
pat
sat
tap
a
at
as

Unit 3
cat
cap
gap
sag
gag
gas

Unit 4
mat
map
it
is
am
sip
in
I

Unit 5
no
nap
nip
tin
on
man
cats
pins

Unit 6
dig
lip
lap
pal
dip
dad
do
did

Unit 8
dog
not
got
log
pot
nod
dot
go
so

Unit 9
bat
big
bin
rob
rip
rod
bad
bag
mob

Unit 10
has
had
an
his
hot
egg
he
she
me

Unit 11
ten
red
bed
get
pet
step
him
my
by

Unit 12
fat
fan
fit
fog
up
us
or
one
fin

Unit 13
of
if
puff
mum
sun
bus
off
hug
put

Unit 14
jam
jog
kid
be
we
the
to
just
are

Unit 16
and
but
too
out
for
her
our
said
you

Unit 17
van
wet
web
yes
zip
zoo
yet
was
will

Unit 18
six
fix
wax
box
fox
axe
went
very
school

Unit 19
miss
less
fuss
hiss
loss
buzz
mess
fizz
class

Unit 20
fry
fly
why
try
cry
sky
this
that
boy

Unit 21
lots
any
many
some
two
how
will

Unit 23
shy
shut
shoe
push
fish
wash
want
have
your

Unit 24
chin
chat
chips
rich
much
such
chess
which
children

Unit 25
back
duck
neck
sick
sock
shock
were
does
what

Unit 26
hill
shall
doll
bell
fell
yell
all
call
full

Unit 27
then
them
they
thick
with
both
three
four
when

Unit 28
sing
hang
long
sang
hung
song
bring
sting
thing

Unit 29
quit
quiz
quick
quack
queen
squash
question
quiet
quite

Unit 31
ate
name
take
safe
eve
these
shake
here
where

Unit 32
like
smile
fine
hope
nose
rude
toe
June
those

Unit 33
see
bee
tree
feet
eat
ear
meat
each
clean

Unit 34
boy
say
joy
boil
sail
join
play
plain
may

Unit 35
how
down
slow
round
found
boat
row
grow
road

Unit 36
food
room
moon
grew
drew
flew
spoon
mood
chew

Spelling Rules! Student Book K (ISBN 9780655092575) © Janelle Ho, Helen Pearson/Matilda Education Australia